the vegan cookbook

DUNCAN BAIRD PUBLISHERS
LONDON

the vegan cookbook

Feed Your Soul, Taste the Love:
100 of the Best Vegan Recipes

Adele McConnell

To my dear husband, Paul.

The Vegan Cookbook
Adele McConnell

First published in the United Kingdom and Ireland
in 2014 by Duncan Baird Publishers, an imprint of
Watkins Publishing Limited
PO Box 883
Oxford, OX1 9PL

A member of Osprey Group

enquiries@dbp.co.uk

Publisher: Grace Cheetham
Editor: Jan Cutler
Art Direction and Design: Manisha Patel
Production: Uzma Taj
Commissioned photography: Keiko Oikawa
Food Stylist: Aya Nishimura
Prop Stylist: Lucy Harvey

A CIP record for this book is available from the
British Library

ISBN: 978-1-84899-104-0

10 9 8 7 6 5 4 3 2 1

Typeset in Nobel, Beton and Biscotti
Colour reproduction by PDQ, UK
Printed in China

PUBLISHER'S NOTE While every care has been taken in
compiling the recipes for this book, Watkins Publishing
Limited, or any other persons who have been involved in
working on this publication, cannot accept responsibility
for any errors or omissions, inadvertent or not, that may be
found in the recipes or text, nor for any problems that may
arise as a result of preparing one of these recipes. If you
are pregnant or breastfeeding or have any special dietary
requirements or medical conditions, it is advisable to
consult a medical professional before following any of
the recipes contained in this book.

NOTES ON THE RECIPES Unless otherwise stated:
• Use filtered water
• Use organic ingredients where possible
• Use home-made vegetable stock in preference, or use
  vegan, gluten-free, dairy-free stock or cubes or granules
• Use medium fruit and vegetables, unless otherwise stated
• Use fresh ingredients, including herbs and chillies
• Do not mix metric and imperial measurements
• 1 tsp = 5ml 1 tbsp = 15ml 1 cup = 250ml

The food symbols refer to the recipes only, not including
ingredient alternatives, optional ingredients or serving
suggestions. Pine nuts and coconut have been classed
as nuts. Coconut sugar has been treated as a nut-free
ingredient, as it is derived from the sap rather than the
nut of the coconut palm.

Check the manufacturer's labelling, because the
ingredients used in different brands vary, especially
for small quantities of ingredients such as soya and
sugar, although manufacturers are not required to
detail minuscule quantities of ingredients.

The 'Raw' symbol has been used to identify recipes
made from raw ingredients that are not heated above
37°C/98.6°F. These recipes may sometimes contain
natural sweeteners such as agave or coconut sugar.
If following a strict raw-foods diet, look for recipes
containing both the 'Sugar-free' and 'Raw' symbols.

Watkins Publishing is supporting the Woodland Trust, the
UK's leading woodland conservation charity, by funding
tree-planting initiatives and woodland maintenance.

www.dbp.co.uk

Contents

Gluten-free

Soya-free

Nut-free

Seed-free

Sugar-free

Raw

Introduction

Writing this book has been the most exciting project I've ever taken on, and it is the result of years of experimentation based on my passion for good, healthy food. I have been blogging on my website, Vegie Head, since 2010, and my recipes have been enjoyed and recreated by tens of thousands of people all over the world, in their homes, in restaurants and in cafés.

There is nothing more satisfying to me than the varied aromas of the food I love: a Mediterranean soup simmering on the stove on a cold day; the fresh smell of home-baked banana bread, still warm from the oven; curry spices being dry-fried, releasing their fragrance, and toasted sesame oil sizzling in a wok.

I was a vegetarian at 17, and I didn't eat eggs or dairy, so after ten years it was an easy step to give up the final few animal foods and become vegan. When I first moved away from home, I wanted to ensure that I was eating and enjoying a wide range of food, so I'd spend my time blending healthy smoothies and making a mess in my yellow 1960's kitchen in Melbourne. I wrote new recipes, amended old recipes to make them vegan, and changed vegan recipes to make them healthier by using coconut oil instead of margarine, home-made almond milk instead of soya milk, and by making green smoothies instead of chocolate 'milkshakes'.

The raw-food movement happened slowly in Australia, but I was hooked immediately. I discovered a whole new way of cooking – or not cooking – and have been excited by the challenge of trying the same foods made in a different way or clever remakes of classics that were enhanced by the health benefits of eating foods raw. Some of my first experiments were with raw cacao powder that I had bought in bulk because I had heard of its health benefits. As a chocolate lover, I have particularly enjoyed trying out new desserts, snacks and smoothies using it.

I don't want to miss out on exciting flavours just because I don't eat animal products, so I focus on delicious food from different cultures.

Whether it's Indian, Moroccan, Thai, Japanese, Vietnamese or Mexican, I've done them all, and I love them all. I adore the earthy spices and the layers of heat in Indian food, and the surprising bursts of sweetness when you bite into a dried fig or a date in Moroccan cuisine. I enjoy the creamy coconut, tangy lemongrass and that zing from kaffir lime that create the signature flavours of Thai dishes. The contrasting textures of Japanese food with its crisp tempura-batter fried vegetables, and the combination of mint and sesame in Vietnamese dishes are all part of my food experience. And then there's the food of Mexico – my beloved. Not the oily, cheese-laden Tex-Mex that is so often passed off as Mexican cooking, but real Mexican food – light, flavoursome and designed to share.

In this book I offer you a fresher, healthier approach to plant-based food – one where you will never have to lose out on flavour and variety. Whatever reason it appeals to you – your concern for animals, consideration for the Earth, or your health – you will find that a plant-based diet is easy and tastes good. You won't be told what you can't eat, but you will probably be introduced to new foods. As you adopt a new diet, you can be an example to those around you. You can change people's perspective on veganism and vegetarianism without scaring them away with statistics, facts or disturbing images, or by listing what they can't do or eat. Instead, you can show them what they can eat and that eating vegan food is an adventure in taste and ingredients.

I mentor hundreds of people all over the world on how to eat a plant-based diet – from athletes and celebrities to your neighbour down the road. They all ask me what they can eat, and they are always surprised by the variety. There is no feeling of deprivation. There is only an abundance of healthy, filling, incredible food.

My way of showing love to those around me is to cook. To be able to bring people together around a table and look into their faces as they savour a mouthful of food made for them is the ultimate act of giving.

For now, feed your soul and taste the love.

The Plant-Based Diet

A diet based on plant foods is not one of restriction or denial. You will find that there is a wide range of healthy and incredibly tasty foods that will make you feel nourished and satisfied after your meals. In the following chapter I explain the benefits of a plant-based diet and how to incorporate plant foods into your daily life. With any change of diet there will be some planning, but when you start on the recipes in this book you can use the more commonly available ingredients. You can then begin to build up a range of healthier alternatives as you become more inspired by this new way of eating.

Variations of Herbed Almond Cheese (page 22) – clockwise from top left: black pepper, apricot, chive, chilli.

The Benefits of Plant Foods

Each one of us is different, and for many people a diet based on plant foods is more suitable than one that is centred on animal produce. It addresses the moral and philosophical objections that many have to eating food from animals, and there are a number of health benefits when you eat only foods made from plants.

THE PLEASURES OF A PLANT-BASED DIET

At the time of writing this book, I have followed a plant-based diet for four years and have never felt better. I sleep well, my digestion is in perfect working order, my skin is clear and my eyes are bright. My hair and nails grow super-fast and I always have tonnes of energy. Many people, through my blog and mentoring sessions, tell me that they have also enjoyed improved health after they have given up meat and animal produce. They are often surprised that a vegan diet can offer such a vast selection of foods and tastes, and they never miss eating meat. They have soon become completely comfortable with, and accustomed to, the fresh flavours of vegetables combined with the more sustaining vegetarian protein foods of pulses and nuts combined with grains.

As you change your diet, you will probably find that the amount of fibre you eat will increase, particularly if you had been following the standard diet of processed foods. Fibre is important for regular bowel motions and managing cholesterol levels. It also stops you from overeating. Processed foods, which are low in fibre, leave you feeling unsatisfied and prone to eating more.

Plants, nuts and seeds are high in vitamins and minerals, and when you eat a variety of them you will increase your body's opportunities to benefit from nutrients and antioxidants that it may never have had in the past. A plant-based diet is low in the type of saturated fat that might be harmful to health, but it does include coconut oil, a saturated fat known as medium chain that your body recognizes as an energy source and uses accordingly. Coconut oil is not easily stored by the body as fat.

Numerous studies have shown that people who eat a plant-based diet have lower rates of heart disease and benefit from lower blood cholesterol levels, lower blood pressure, a lower incidence of type-2 diabetes and lower rates of prostate and colon cancer, according to the American Dietetic Association.

Health benefits aside, a plant-based diet can widen your horizons for discovering a wealth of new flavours, textures, colours, tastes and culinary experiences.

RAW INGREDIENTS FOR A HEALTH BOOST

Eating some foods raw and unprocessed – in smoothies, salads, and even dessert cakes – is a great way to experiment with new, nutrient-packed ingredients. By including raw foods in your diet you will benefit from those minerals and nutrients that are lost when food is cooked or heated above 37°C/98.6°F. There are a number of raw recipes in the book. Look for the 'Raw' symbol.

A RELEASE FROM SOME OF THE STRESSES IN LIFE

For me, one of the benefits of not eating animal foods is that I won't be a part of the stress that animals go through at the end of their lives – and all too frequently while being reared as well. When you eat meat, chicken or fish, you are eating those creatures' fear. You are consuming their stress, their hormones and, metaphysically, their energy.

I have realized that in order for me to live as stress-free a life as possible, I need to appreciate the intimate relationship that food has with the body, mind and spirit. Clearing my body of animal produce has allowed me to tap into a deeper level of consciousness and to have more compassion for other living beings.

CHOOSING A MEAT-FREE LIFESTYLE

One way to decide which kind of diet you might like to follow is to ask yourself, 'Is this food serving me? Is this food helping me to reach my full, healthy potential? Is what I'm about to eat good for me and for the world?' You may then decide that following a vegan, or at least a meat-free, lifestyle is the right choice for you.

Plant-Based Foods for Every Day of Your Life

I explain to my clients that there are no good or bad foods when you follow a plant-based diet, but it's more about adding new ingredients to your selection and discovering the benefits of eating more raw produce. As your choices widen, so will the nutritional value of your daily diet. When you increase the good things, the less-beneficial foods take a back seat.

THE FIRST STEPS

Rather than banning foods, start to introduce new ones – for example, add almond milk to your cereal every day, and handfuls of kale or spinach to your stir-fries, pastas and soups. With just those few changes you will have increased the amount of fibre, vitamins, minerals and nutrients in your diet without really changing anything else.

If you have always drunk dairy milk, you might find nut milks a little unusual to start with, but you'll soon get to like the fresh non-dairy taste. You can make nut milks yourself, and I include a recipe in this book. Try different types of nut until you find a flavour you like.

If you can, shop at your local health-food shop, organic or local greengrocer, or farmers' market – or even at the fresh aisles in the supermarket, keeping away from the convenience foods. Stock up on foods such as brown rice. It is satisfying, wholesome and makes a great base for meals such as curries and stews. Lentils and cannellini beans – and a wide range of other pulses – are delicious added to soups and casseroles and are an inexpensive way to bulk meals and add protein.

I choose not to use a lot of soya in my diet, but I have included some tofu and tempeh recipes in this book due to popular demand. Soya contains phytoestrogens – plant hormones that mimic oestrogen in the body. Some experts claim that too much soya can be detrimental to health, so I suggest that if you choose to eat it, have it in moderation and preferably use fermented soya (miso, tempeh and tamari), which is easier to digest. I also prefer to use coconut sugar or coconut nectar rather than cane sugar. They have a lower glycaemic index (GI) and do not cause a rapid increase in blood sugar levels (sugar spikes), which encourage weight gain and lead to unhealthy conditions in the body, such as diabetes.

CHOOSE PROTEIN AND NUTRIENT-RICH FOODS

Animal proteins are called complete proteins because they contain all the essential amino acids that the body cannot produce itself. Soya foods are also complete proteins. Plant foods have different amino-acid profiles, so vegans need to eat a variety of grains, pulses, nuts and seeds to meet the body's needs. These don't all have to be included in the same meal but can be eaten over the course of a day.

Eat flaxseeds and chia seeds to obtain your omega-3 essential fats. It's also important to ensure that you have sufficient vitamin B12, which is not available from plant foods. To do this, take a B12 supplement or choose fortified foods (some soya products are fortified), or add B12-fortified nutritional yeast flakes to food. Not all nutritional yeast flakes contain B12, however, so you need to check the pack.

MAKE DISCOVERIES

Be adventurous and try new and foreign foods. Many foods that might seem new to you may actually have a very long history in other parts of the world and sustained people for perhaps thousands of years. Antioxidant-rich cacao, protein-packed quinoa and omega-3-rich chia seeds, for example, are ancient foods from South America with healthy properties that have only recently been fully understood elsewhere.

In this book you'll find plenty of ways to use a variety of foods that are full of health benefits. Most are available from health-food shops and many can be bought in supermarkets. In the next section I list the storecupboard foods to search out, explain why they make healthy choices, how to use them and what to use as alternatives.

The Vegan Storecupboard

You can stock up your storecupboard (or pantry, as we call it in Australia) gradually. I love to visit speciality stores, international delis and markets to buy spices, condiments and ingredients, and then make a dish taste new by adding a different spice or flavouring from my growing selection.

To save costs, I buy a lot of my pulses (peas, beans and lentils) in bulk, as well as almonds and cashew nuts to make 'milks' and raw desserts. (You could also share a bulk buy with a friend.) For taste and health reasons, everything I eat is organic, and I recommend you do the same. I stock up with fresh, organic fruit and vegetables at least once a week.

Most of the ingredients in this book are easy to find and you can substitute the more unusual ones with readily available alternatives. I have chosen to use healthy ingredients in this cookbook, because these are what I eat. You'll still be able to make most of the recipes without them though. The more exotic ingredients can usually be found at a well-stocked health-food shop, and all can be purchased from online stockists, if necessary.

Some of the foods listed below may be unfamiliar, but are chosen for their health benefits. Alternatives are given, but where possible gradually try to increase the healthier versions in your own storecupboard. As mentioned earlier, I choose to limit my soya intake. Soya is found in many things, not just soya milk, and is often labelled as lecithin (soya based), hydrolyzed soya protein (HSP), MSG (monosodium glutamate), mono- and di-glycerides, among others.

Almonds High in magnesium, vitamin E, phosphorus and calcium, almonds are a great convenience snack and they make incredible milk.
Antipasti vegetables Sun-dried tomatoes and artichokes stored in oil in jars (or artichokes in brine from a tin), are handy to add to a tomato-based pasta sauce for a quick and easy dinner or to serve on a platter with vegan cheese and biscuits.
Cacao nibs are shelled and crushed cacao beans. They have a dark, bitter taste, and a small amount will add a chocolatey flavour to any dish. This is *real*, unprocessed chocolate, containing feel-good nutrients

such as theobromine, phenylethylamine and anandamide. If you don't have raw cacao nibs or raw cacao powder, a high-quality vegan dark chocolate will suffice.

Cacao powder is made from raw, ground cacao beans and has a fairly bitter, rich and earthy taste. Rich in magnesium and antioxidants, it is a healthier choice than cocoa, which is highly processed and has lost much of the nutritional value that was present in the raw product. You can use cocoa instead of cacao, but not if you are making a raw recipe.

Carob powder Carob, a legume (bean), has a mildly sweet and fruity taste. Unlike chocolate, it contains no caffeine. The powder can be used in place of cacao or cocoa in recipes. Milder-flavoured raw carob has not been heat treated and is preferable for raw desserts.

Chia seeds are ancient Mexican seeds that have recently been gaining recognition because of their healthy properties. They are high in the essential fatty acids, omega-3 and -6, and they are useful for vegans because they contain vital omega-3, which is difficult to obtain from animal-free sources. Chia seeds can be added to smoothies, cereals, baked products, soups and salads. They also make an egg replacer for binding by soaking in 1 or 2 tablespoons water until they form a gel.

Coconut aminos is similar to soy sauce, but without the soya. It is less salty, but it still has the same kick you expect from soy sauce or tamari. It can be used in place of both.

Coconut cream is the thick, solid layer that forms on the top of coconut milk, if the fat content is high enough, and is also sold as cream in cartons and tins. For extra-thick cream, store the carton or tin upright in the fridge, then open it and take off the cream from the top.

Coconut milk is a more liquid equivalent of coconut cream. The thickness and quality of milk varies according to the brand. I choose cream most of the time and water it down myself if I need milk.

Coconut nectar is a mineral-rich liquid from the sap of coconut trees. It has a caramel-butterscotch flavour and can be used in place of honey, agave syrup, and any plain sugar product. It has a low GI, and it also contains vitamin C.

Coconut oil has a fairly high smoke point (176°C/350°F), and so is suitable for frying. It can be heated without being damaged and oxidized, as other oils are. Oxidization causes oils to become unhealthy free radicals in the body. Choose organic, virgin and unrefined coconut oil, which is minimally processed. Non-virgin coconut oil may be produced from dried coconut (copra) and will have lost nutrients as well as being highly processed. Use coconut oil for baking, frying and in desserts or smoothies.

Alternatively, use OLIVE OIL (not extra virgin) for frying over medium heat. Organic SAFFLOWER OIL is high in omega-6 essential fats and is my personal alternative for cooking if I am short of coconut oil. RICE BRAN OIL is rich in vitamin E and omega-6, and has a high smoke point at 232°C/ 450°F. The only oil suitable for raw dishes, however, is coconut oil – for taste, nutrition and its ability to solidify quickly.

Coconut sugar Compared to cane sugar, coconut sugar has a lower GI. It is also rich in minerals and its mild caramel taste makes it a good alternative to cane sugar. You can make the recipes in this book using brown sugar, but try to source coconut sugar to make sweet dishes healthier if you can. Coconut sugar is classed as raw, so it is used instead of brown sugar for recipes in this book that are labelled as raw. AGAVE SYRUP is sometimes given as a sweetener, although I rarely use it because it is high in fructose, which can lead to weight gain. BROWN RICE SYRUP is my preferred alternative as a sweetening syrup.

Coconut yogurt A relative newcomer to the market, dairy-free coconut yogurt is a wonderful substitute for soya yogurt. It is rich and creamy and has the most amazing taste. Store it in the fridge.

Desiccated coconut and coconut flakes are nutritious and useful for adding to cakes, muffins and smoothies.

Dried fruits Providing they are organic and sulphur-free, dried fruits, such as cherries, cranberries, apricots and dates, can be used in a number of dishes. (See also Medjool dates, below.)

Gluten-free flour is available in a variety of types, such as brown rice, coconut, buckwheat and gram (chickpea). Your local health-food shop or supermarket should stock a range, and you can also buy gluten-free flour blends, although these vary in quality. All gluten-free flours work slightly differently from regular flour and I recommend you try different ones to see which you prefer. Coconut flour is a tricky ingredient to work with because it absorbs a lot of liquid. If you try it, use only 20–30 per cent of the quantity of the regular flour stated in the recipe.

Goji berries These nutrient-rich fruits can taste both tart and sweet. Use them in smoothies, salads, raw desserts and curries.

Grains Whole grains contain fibre and minerals that are lost when grains are processed. Use grains, such as quinoa, brown rice and polenta, in place of white pasta. Quinoa and brown rice are also good for bulking up soups, salads and even breakfasts.

Green super-foods include SPIRULINA – a green sea algae that is high in protein and vitamins – and BARLEY GRASS/WHEATGRASS – a highly alkalizing product that can help balance the acid/alkaline levels in the body. They are not essential for the recipes, and are quite pricey, but I feel they benefit my energy, skin and eyes.

Maca is a Peruvian root that may balance hormones. It has a fruity taste and can be added to raw desserts, smoothies and hot drinks.

Medjool dates Dates are high in fibre and a natural sweetener, which makes them useful to add to smoothies and raw desserts instead of using sugar or a syrup. I use fresh medjool dates in recipes because they are large and soft, but you can use dried dates, although sometimes you may need to soak them first.

Miso is a fermented soya product, also containing rice or barley, and can be beneficial to the digestion. Miso is salty and makes a great base for soups and Asian dishes. You can purchase dried miso for your storecupboard, but miso paste should be stored in the fridge.

Nutritional yeast flakes have a cheesy flavour and are bright yellow in colour. Add them to soups, stews or pasta, or use them to make a vegan cheese sauce (page 23). They contain B vitamins, and some brands are high in essential B12, a bacterium found easily in animal products, so are useful for vegans.

Nut butters Raw nut butters are a delicious, fresh alternative to regular bought peanut butter. You can make them yourself if you have a powerful blender. Almond butter, cashew butter and pecan butter are my favourites, but you can also make butters with macadamia nuts, hazelnuts and walnuts. Use them as you would regular peanut butter, add them to smoothies and raw desserts or eat straight from the jar.

Nuts are a great way to get protein into a vegan diet (don't be scared by the fat content). They contain healthy fats when eaten raw and unprocessed. You can add a variety to your diet, such as almonds, macadamia nuts, hazelnuts, pecan and pistachio nuts, walnuts and peanuts (which are actually a legume, although we still eat them as a nut). Eat them alone, in salads, soups and stews, in raw desserts and smoothies, or blend them into nut butters.

Olives Add black or green olives to pasta, salads and antipasti for a delicious salty kick.

Pulses The high protein content of pulses makes them important in the vegan diet. They are also rich in amino acids – the body's building blocks. Lentils, kidney beans, chickpeas, broad beans and butter beans are pulses that are cheap to buy, convenient to use and make a dish filling and sustaining. Dried red lentils cook in just 20 minutes, and many other pulses can be bought ready-cooked in tins.

Seaweeds are rich in iodine and offer a broad range of other nutrients: B vitamins, folate, magnesium, iron, calcium and riboflavin. Salty-flavoured NORI sheets are used to make hand-rolls. AGAR-AGAR is used to set jellies and desserts in a similar way to the animal product, gelatine.

Seeds High in protein and minerals, sesame, pumpkin, sunflower and flaxseeds are just a few of the healthy seeds available. You can sprinkle them on salads and soups, and make them into milks.

Soya products Soya is a good way for vegans to get protein into their diets, but look for non-GM and organic brands. TOFU can be used in savoury and sweet dishes due to its bland taste and colour, and its ability to absorb other flavours. TEMPEH is a nutty-tasting fermented soya product, which needs to be cooked before eating.

Soy sauces Salty-flavoured soy sauce and tamari are made from fermented soya beans. TAMARI is gluten-free, and both can be used interchangeably in many recipes.

Tahini, made from sesame seeds, is protein-rich and, when raw, is high in vitamins E, B1, B2 and A.

Tinned/packaged foods Where possible, choose organic versions of passata, tinned tomatoes and pulses. Avoid tins that are lined with the toxic plastic bisphenol A (BPA).

SPICES AND FLAVOURINGS

Good basics for spicy dishes include dried cumin, coriander, turmeric and cinnamon, plus dried and crushed chillies, and also always have some fresh chillies in the fridge. For an authentic touch, try:

Chermoula paste A mixture of herbs, spices, oil and lemon used in Moroccan dishes. Add it to tagines or to vegetables before roasting.

Galangal A root with an aromatic, peppery flavour.

Garam masala A mixture of Indian spices, predominantly cinnamon, cumin, peppercorns, cloves and cardamom.

Harissa A hot and spicy chilli paste used in North African cooking.

Kaffir lime leaves, which lend a tang and fragrance to Thai cooking. Freeze fresh leaves for up to 8 months in a freezer bag.

Lemongrass to give Thai and Asian cooking that distinctive flavour. Buy it fresh and store it in the fridge.

Mirin A low-alcohol Japanese rice wine, with a sweet 'kick'. It can transform the flavour of a stir-fry.

Paprika, either sweet or smoked, adds a deep level of flavour and aroma to dishes, particularly those from Mexico and Morocco.

Rice wine vinegar to add depth of flavour to Asian dishes.

Tamarind is used in Asian cooking for its sweet, sour and tangy flavour.

Vanilla The seeds of vanilla pods are used widely in this book. Use the pods to flavour sugar. Vanilla bean paste is a convenient way to get the flavour of vanilla from a pod without the effort.

You can also use cashew nuts, macadamia nuts, hazelnuts or sesame seeds to create your own dairy-free milks.

almond milk

Makes: 750ml/26fl oz/3 cups
Preparation: 15 minutes, plus
  overnight soaking

150g/5½oz/1 cup almonds
  with skins

OPTIONAL
1 vanilla pod
2 fresh or dried medjool
  dates, pitted

Put the almonds in a bowl, cover with water and leave to soak overnight. Drain in a colander and rinse well, then drain again. If using the vanilla pod, split the pod in half lengthways and scrape out the seeds. Reserve the pod for another use.

Put the almonds into a blender or food processor with 500ml/17fl oz/2 cups water and the vanilla seeds and dates, if using. Blend on high speed for 1–2 minutes. Check the consistency. If you prefer your milk thinner, add up to 250ml/9fl oz/1 cup water and pulse to combine.

Strain through a nut-milk bag, or a fine sieve or muslin. (The almonds can be drip-dried for a wetter pulp – perfect for making cheese. Put the bag filled with pulp on to an upturned saucer inside a larger bowl and put a heavy weight, such as a tin of beans, on a small plate on top of the bag.)

Reserve the pulp for later use (see Herbed Almond Cheese, page 22). The milk can be stored in a sealed glass jar in the fridge for up to 4 days, and can also be frozen in ice-cube trays and the cubes stored in freezer bags for up to 2 months.

Gluten-free   Soya-free   Seed-free   Sugar-free   Raw

white cottage-feta cheese

Makes: 160g/5¾oz
Preparation: 20 minutes, plus
overnight soaking and an
optional overnight pressing

160g/5¾oz/1 cup
  macadamia nuts
30g/1oz/¼ cup pitted green
  olives, chopped
1 tsp grated lemon zest
juice of 1 lemon
½ tsp crushed chillies
  (optional)
¼ tsp freshly ground
  black pepper
sea salt

Put the macadamia nuts in a bowl, cover with water and leave to soak overnight. Drain in a colander, then rinse well and drain again.

Put the macadamia nuts into a blender or food processor with 125ml/4fl oz/½ cup water. Blend into a fine paste. Using a nut-milk bag, or a fine sieve or muslin, squeeze out the excess water.

Stir in the olives, lemon zest and juice, crushed chillies, if using, and pepper, then add salt to taste. The cheese should be white, with a cottage-cheese consistency, but it should be salty like feta. The cheese is ready to eat straightaway or it can be pressed to make it firm. To do this, wrap the cheese in muslin and put it on a plate. Put a heavy weight, such as a tin of beans, on a small plate on top of the cheese and leave overnight.

Gluten-free   Soya-free   Seed-free   Sugar-free   Raw

You can use leftover Almond Milk pulp (page 20) here, but without soaking and processing the almonds. Vary the herbs, if you like (but don't add the onion and garlic if using coriander), or use 2 chopped chillies, 1½ tablespoons ground black pepper or 80g/2¾oz chopped ready-to-eat dried apricots. Try rolling the cheese in herbs or coarsely ground peppercorns.

herbed almond cheese

Makes: 500g/1lb 2oz
Preparation: 25 minutes, plus
overnight soaking, 4 hours
fermenting, 3 hours chilling

300g/10½oz/2 cups almonds
with skins
½ red onion, chopped
1 garlic clove, crushed
1 tsp lemon juice
1 small handful of parsley
leaves, finely chopped
2 tsp miso
1 tbsp finely chopped dill
freshly ground black pepper

Put the almonds in a bowl, cover with water and leave to soak overnight. Drain in a colander, then rinse well and drain again. If you like, you can remove the skins by rubbing them with a dry tea towel. (If you remove the skins you will have a sweeter-flavoured cheese.)

Put the almonds into a blender or food processor and add 250ml/9fl oz/1 cup water. Blend until smooth and then strain through a nut-milk bag, or a fine sieve or muslin.

Roll the pulp into a ball and put it back into the nut-milk bag, then put the bag in a bowl. Put a heavy weight, such as a tin of beans, on a small plate on top of the bag of pulp and leave to ferment for 3–4 hours.

Put the strained almond pulp back into the blender, and add the onion, garlic and lemon juice. Season with pepper, then process until well combined. Tip into a bowl and add the parsley, miso and dill. Mix well, then roll into a ball. Chill in the fridge for 3 hours before serving.

Gluten-free   *Seed-free*   *Sugar-free*   *Raw*

Nutritional yeast flakes give this savoury sauce a rich, cheese-like flavour. Use the sauce in lasagne, with pasta or as a dip for lightly steamed vegetables.

vegan cheese sauce

**Makes: about 560ml/
  19¼fl oz/2¼ cups
Preparation: 15 minutes,
  plus 30 minutes soaking
Cooking: 15 minutes**

150g/5½oz/1 cup cashew
  nuts
500ml/17fl oz/2 cups rice
  milk
70g/2½oz/1½ cups
  nutritional yeast flakes
1 tsp miso, soy sauce or
  tamari soy sauce
juice of ½ lemon
1 tbsp rice flour or plain flour
freshly ground black pepper

Put the cashew nuts in a bowl, cover with water and leave to soak for 30 minutes. Drain the cashew nuts in a colander and put them into a blender or food processor, then process until fine.

Pour the milk into a medium saucepan over a medium heat and add 250ml/9fl oz/1 cup water. Whisk together and bring gently to the boil, then reduce the heat to a simmer.

Add the yeast flakes, ground cashew nuts, miso, lemon juice and flour. Season with pepper and whisk until smooth. The sauce will thicken after a minute or so. Once thickened, remove from the heat and serve or use in your chosen recipe.

Seed-free   *Sugar-free*

Use this versatile, fresh tomato sauce as a base for a vegetable sauce with nuts, pulses or tempeh to serve over pasta or grains. Or serve it with polenta, pies or the Red Lentil & Beetroot Burgers (page 148) instead of the relish and buns.

tomato sauce

**Makes: about 2l/70fl oz/
  8 cups**
Preparation: 25 minutes
Cooking: 3½ hours

5kg/11lb plum tomatoes or
  other ripe tomatoes
1 tbsp olive oil or safflower
  oil
1 garlic bulb, cloves crushed
4 onions, thinly sliced
1 handful of basil leaves,
  chopped
1 tsp brown sugar or coconut
  sugar, plus extra if needed
sea salt and freshly ground
  black pepper

Cut the tomatoes in half and cut out the cores, then roughly chop the flesh. Put the tomatoes in a pan over a medium heat and cook for 20 minutes, stirring occasionally, so that the tomatoes release their juice – they do not need any added water.

Heat the oil in a shallow saucepan over a medium heat and cook the garlic and onions for 5–8 minutes until softened.

Tip the onion mixture into the tomatoes and add the basil, then stir well. Using a blender or food processor, blend the mixture until smooth. You may have to do this in batches.

Add 1 teaspoon sugar and 1 teaspoon salt, then taste. If the sauce is too tart, add more sugar. If the sauce is too sweet, add more salt. Add pepper to taste.

Simmer the sauce over a medium heat for 3 hours, or until reduced and thick. Serve, or add to your recipe, or leave to cool. Once cold, the sauce can be transferred to sterilized jars and stored for up to 4 days in the fridge or divided into 250ml/9fl oz/1 cup portions and frozen in freezer bags for up to 2 months.

Gluten-free   *Soya-free*   *Nut-free*   *Seed-free*

Traditionally, this paste is pounded, ingredient by ingredient, using a mortar and pestle, but my faster version uses a blender. Use either red or green chillies to change the colour and heat of the paste – bird's eye chillies have the best flavour.

thai red or green curry paste

**Makes: about 125ml/4fl oz/
½ cup**
Preparation: 15 minutes
Cooking: 5 minutes

1 tsp coriander seeds
1 tsp white peppercorns
2 lemongrass stalks, outer leaves and stalk removed, white part only
3 shallots
10 garlic cloves
2.5cm/1in piece fresh root ginger, peeled
2.5cm/1in piece galangal, peeled, or 1cm/½in piece fresh root ginger, peeled
grated zest of 1 lime, preferably kaffir lime
5–10 hot red chillies, preferably bird's eye, or milder green chillies, tops trimmed
juice of 1 lime
1 large handful of coriander roots, stems and leaves

Put the coriander seeds and white peppercorns in a small pan and toast over a medium heat for 3 minutes, shaking the pan frequently, to release the aroma. Remove from the heat.

Put all the ingredients into a blender or food processor and blend into a paste. Use immediately or store in the fridge for up to 1 week. The paste can also be frozen in ice-cube trays and the cubes stored in freezer bags for up to 2 months.

Gluten-free   *Soya-free*   *Nut-free*   *Seed-free*   *Sugar-free*

fruit & pumpkin spread

**Makes: about 1kg/2lb 4oz/
  3 cups**
Preparation: 20 minutes
Cooking: 1 hour 10 minutes

6 apricots or 3 peaches, cut
  in half and pitted
300g/10½oz pumpkin or
  butternut squash, peeled
  and cut into cubes
4 large pears or apples,
  peeled, cored and cut
  into dice
180g/6¼oz/1 cup brown
  sugar or coconut sugar
1 tsp ground cinnamon
½ tsp ground cardamom
½ tsp ground ginger
½ tsp ground allspice

Put all the ingredients in a large, heavy-based saucepan and add
185ml/6fl oz/¾ cup water, then combine well.

Bring to the boil over a medium heat, then reduce the heat to low
and simmer for 1 hour, stirring frequently, or until the pumpkin
and fruit are soft. Add extra water if the mixture starts to catch
on the base of the pan. Pour the mixture into a blender or food
processor and blend until smooth. Serve or cool and store in a
covered container in the fridge for up to 7 days.

Gluten-free   Soya-free   Nut-free   Seed-free

chocolate & hazelnut butter

Makes: 625g/1lb 6oz/2½ cups
Preparation: 10 minutes

1 vanilla pod
280g/10oz/2 cups hazelnuts
30g/1oz/⅓ cup raw cacao
  powder
80ml/2½fl oz/⅓ cup brown
  rice syrup or agave syrup
a pinch of sea salt

Split the vanilla pod in half lengthways and scrape out the seeds.
Reserve the pod for another use. Leave the seeds to one side.
Put the hazelnuts in a blender or food processor and grind until
smooth. Continue to grind until the nuts become butter. Add the
cacao powder, syrup, vanilla seeds and salt. Pulse to combine.
Serve or store in a sterilized jar in the fridge for up to 2 weeks.

Gluten-free   Soya-free   Seed-free   Raw

Home-made Indian breads are fast and easy to make, and they taste very good indeed. You can make them by hand or using a food processor while your curry is simmering.

garlic parathas

Makes: 8 parathas
Preparation: 20 minutes,
 plus 10 minutes resting
Cooking: 15 minutes

300g/10½oz/2 cups
 wholemeal flour, plus extra
 for dusting
2 tbsp good-quality olive oil
a pinch of sea salt
2 garlic cloves, crushed

Preheat the oven to 100°C/200°F/Gas ½ and put a heatproof plate inside to warm.

Sift the flour into a large bowl, tipping in any bran left in the sieve, and add the remaining ingredients and 125ml/4fl oz/ ½ cup lukewarm water. Stir well to combine thoroughly, then turn out on to a floured work surface. Knead for 2 minutes, or until the dough is smooth and springy, and then put it in a floured bowl and leave to one side to rest for 10 minutes. (Alternatively, if you have a food processor with a kneading attachment, add all the ingredients and knead until the dough combines.)

Heat a non-stick frying pan over a medium heat. Divide the dough into 8 pieces and flatten them with your hands. Working carefully to retain the stretchy dough, flatten one piece with a rolling pin, then put it in the hot frying pan. Cook for 1 minute, then turn it over, using a palette knife. Cook for a further 1 minute, then press down with a clean, dry, tea towel to ensure the paratha cooks evenly.

Wrap the paratha in foil and keep warm in the oven while you cook the remaining dough, or serve each paratha as soon as it comes out of the frying pan.

Soya-free   Nut-free   Seed-free   Sugar-free

Breakfasts & Brunches

Often called the most important meal of the day, breakfast should be nourishing and appealing with plenty of variety. There are tempting breakfasts here for every day of the week. Long brunches and lazy breakfasts can be on everyone's weekend menu, because all the recipes here are fast to prepare, and some can be left to cook slowly, such as the Breakfast Tagine, giving you maximum weekend relaxation with minimal effort. Weekdays are simple as well. You will find a smoothie to go, or a fruit salad with a twist. A Chocolate Mudslide Smoothie will kick-start your day, and my Watermelon & Orange Salad will freshen you up. Some breakfasts can even be made in advance – try Peanut Butter & Banana Bread, Tea-Poached Prunes or Toasted Granola. Throw some breakfast together and let the good days roll.

Over-the-Top Banana
Oatmeal (page 41).

peach passion smoothie

Serves: 2
Preparation: 10 minutes,
plus making the milk

4 ripe peaches, cut into
   quarters and pitted
2 passion fruits, cut in half
   and flesh scooped out
650ml/22fl oz/2½ cups
   Almond Milk (page 20)
1 large handful of ice cubes
1 fresh or dried medjool date,
   pitted
1 tsp coconut oil (optional)
fresh mint leaves, to serve

Put all the ingredients into a blender or food processor and
blend at high speed until smooth and creamy. Serve in tall
glasses and decorate with fresh mint leaves.

Gluten-free   *Soya-free*   *Seed-free*   *Sugar-free*   *Raw*

chocolate mudslide smoothie

Serves: 2
Preparation: 10 minutes,
plus overnight freezing
and making the milk

2 bananas, peeled and
   chopped
2 tbsp raw cacao powder
1 tbsp cacao nibs
1 tbsp carob powder
650ml/22fl oz/2½ cups
   Almond Milk (page 20)
1 tsp ground cinnamon
1 tsp maca powder (optional)
1 tsp spirulina (optional)
desiccated coconut, to serve

Put the bananas in a freezer bag, seal and freeze overnight. Put
all the ingredients into a blender or food processor and blend
at high speed until smooth and creamy. Top with desiccated
coconut to serve.

Gluten-free   *Soya-free*   *Seed-free*   *Sugar-free*   *Raw*

black forest *smoothie*

Serves: 2
Preparation: 10 minutes,
  plus making the milk

1 vanilla pod
750ml/26fl oz/3 cups
  Almond Milk (page 20)
225g/8oz/1 cup fresh or
  frozen cherries, pitted
2 tbsp raw cacao powder
1 tbsp carob powder
1 tbsp almond butter
1½ tsp ground cinnamon
2 fresh or dried medjool
  dates, pitted
1 tbsp chia seeds

Split the vanilla pod in half lengthways and scrape out the seeds. Reserve the pod for another use. Put the seeds into a blender or food processor and add the remaining ingredients. Blend until smooth and creamy, then serve immediately.

Gluten-free *Soya-free* *Sugar-free* *Raw*

cucumber, lime & *watermelon juice*

Serves: 2
Preparation: 10 minutes

2 cucumbers, cut into
  quarters
1 lime, peeled and cut into
  quarters
550g/1lb 4 oz watermelon,
  roughly chopped
1 handful of fresh mint
  leaves, chopped
ice cubes, to serve

Put the cucumbers, lime and watermelon through an electric juicer. Add the mint and serve over ice. (Alternatively, juice the mint with the other ingredients, if you like.)

Gluten-free *Soya-free* *Nut-free* *Seed-free* *Sugar-free* *Raw*

The cooling and sweet watermelon in this breakfast salad is set off by tangy orange and lime. It's high in soluble fibre, antioxidants and vitamin C, as well as beta-carotene and potassium, making it a perfect way to start the day.

watermelon & *orange salad*

Serves: 2
Preparation: 15 minutes,
  plus 30 minutes chilling

1 orange
550g/1lb 4oz watermelon,
  cut into slices
1 small cucumber, cut in half
  and thinly sliced
2 tbsp lime juice
1 tbsp mint leaves
grated zest of 1 lime
dairy-free yogurt, to serve
  (optional)

Using a sharp knife, cut a thin slice of peel and pith from each end of the orange. Put the orange cut-side down on a plate and cut off the peel and pith in strips. Remove any remaining pith. Cut out each segment, leaving the membrane behind.

Put the orange in a serving bowl, then squeeze in the remaining juice from the membrane. Add the watermelon, cucumber, lime juice and mint, then toss together. Sprinkle with lime zest, then cover and chill in the fridge for 30 minutes to allow the flavours to develop. Serve with dairy-free yogurt, if you like.

Gluten-free   Soya-free   Nut-free   Seed-free   Sugar-free   Raw

In this recipe, the sweetness of the prunes is offset by the floral bergamot and tannins from the Earl Grey tea they are poached in. This is a simple breakfast that can be prepared the night before – and it keeps for a few days.

tea-poached *prunes*

Serves: 6
Preparation: 5 minutes, plus
  overnight chilling and
  making the granola

270g/9½ oz/2 cups ready-to-eat pitted prunes
125ml/4fl oz/½ cup orange juice
500ml/17fl oz/2 cups freshly brewed Earl Grey tea or English tea
Toasted Granola (page 36) and dairy-free yogurt, to serve

Put the prunes in a bowl and pour over the orange juice and tea. Leave to one side to cool, then cover and chill in the fridge overnight.

To serve, spoon the prunes and tea syrup over the granola and top with a spoonful of yogurt. Store the soaked prunes in a covered container in the fridge for up to 4 days.

Gluten-free *Soya-free* *Nut-free* *Seed-free* *Sugar-free*

The options are endless for added toppings to this banana breakfast or dessert – hazelnuts, cranberries, fresh strawberries or raspberries and sliced oranges to name just a few, apart from the selection below. You can also make this into a smoothie by blending everything together, including the liquid from the carton of coconut cream.

banana split with coconut cream whip

Serves: 2
**Preparation: 15 minutes,
    plus overnight chilling**

250ml/9fl oz/1 cup coconut cream in the unopened carton or tin
2 bananas
1 tsp vanilla paste or vanilla extract
1 tbsp cacao nibs or chopped dark vegan chocolate
1 tbsp goji berries or dried cranberries
1 tbsp flaked almonds
1 tsp pumpkin seeds
1 tsp sunflower seeds
1 tsp carob powder, cocoa powder or raw cacao powder
1 tsp ground cinnamon

Chill the coconut cream overnight in the fridge, making sure the carton is upright. Without shaking the carton, open it and scoop off the cream from the top. It will be very, very thick. Put the cream into a blender or food processor and leave the coconut liquid to one side.

Peel the bananas and cut them in half lengthways, then put two halves in each of two serving bowls.

Add the vanilla to the blender. Pour in some of the reserved coconut liquid, 1 tablespoon at a time, while blending for 2–3 minutes until the coconut cream is soft but thick enough to hold its shape. Spoon on to the split bananas, and top with the cacao nibs, goji berries, almonds, and pumpkin and sunflower seeds. Dust with carob powder and cinnamon, then serve.

Gluten-free *Soya-free* *Sugar-free*

Soya-free

toasted *granola*

Serves: 6
Preparation: 15 minutes,
  plus making the milk
  and optional prunes
Cooking: 20 minutes,
  plus cooling

250g/9oz/2½ cups rolled
  oats
250g/9oz/2 cups seed
  and grain mix (sesame,
  pumpkin, sunflower, rye,
  barley, bran)
150g/5½oz/1 cup almonds,
  chopped
100g/3½oz/1 cup pecan
  nuts, roughly chopped
125ml/4fl oz/½ cup safflower
  oil, sunflower oil or melted
  coconut oil
50g/1¾oz/¼ cup brown
  sugar or coconut sugar
2 tsp ground cinnamon
Almond Milk (page 20) and
  fresh fruit, or Tea-Poached
  Prunes (page 34), to serve

Preheat the oven to 160°C/315°F/Gas 2½ and line a baking
tray with baking parchment. Put the oats in a large bowl and
add the seed and grain mixture, almonds and pecan nuts.

Put the oil in a small bowl and add the sugar and cinnamon.
Whisk together, then drizzle over the oat mixture. Stir well to
ensure the oat mixture is thoroughly coated. Spread out evenly
on the prepared baking tray and bake for 10 minutes, then shake
the mixture and bake for a further 10 minutes. Leave to cool,
then serve with almond milk and fresh fruit. Store in a sterilized
glass jar, in a cool dry place, for up to 3 weeks.

Gluten-free Soya-free Seed-free

quinoa porridge with rhubarb & *apple compote*

**Serves: 2 (with compote
  left over)**
**Preparation: 15 minutes,
  plus cooling and making
  the milk**
Cooking: 40 minutes

100g/3½oz/½ cup quinoa,
  rinsed and drained
500ml/17fl oz/2 cups
  Almond Milk (page 20),
  plus extra to serve
1 tbsp brown sugar or
  coconut sugar
1 tbsp vanilla extract
1 tsp ground cinnamon

RHUBARB AND APPLE COMPOTE
450g/1lb rhubarb, chopped
2 apples, peeled, cored and
  cut into dice
60g/2¼oz/⅓ cup brown
  sugar or coconut sugar

To make the compote, put all the ingredients in a medium saucepan and add 125ml/4fl oz/½ cup water. Combine well and bring to the boil over a medium heat, then reduce the heat to low. Make sure that the rhubarb and apples are completely submerged. Stir to dissolve the sugar. Simmer for 10–15 minutes, until the rhubarb is soft.

Leave the compote to cool completely, then pour into a sterilized glass jar. Store in the fridge for 1 week, or divide into portions in freezer bags and freeze for up to 1 month.

To make the porridge, put the quinoa in a heavy-based saucepan and add the milk, sugar, vanilla and cinnamon. Stir well to combine, then bring to a gentle boil over a medium heat. Cook for 20 minutes, stirring occasionally, or until the quinoa is tender and translucent and the porridge has thickened. Serve with a dash of milk, and some of the compote. (The compote can also be served with ice cream, in smoothies or spread on pancakes.)

Served in a tall glass, this looks more like a dessert than a breakfast. The oatmeal can be made the night before. If you like, add some chia seeds to your yogurt to include some healthy omega-3 and -6 fats, plus more fibre and protein.

over-the-top banana *oatmeal*

Serves: 2
Preparation: 20 minutes,
  plus cooling and 1 hour or
  overnight chilling, and
  making the milk
Cooking: 20 minutes

60g/2¼oz/⅔ cup rolled oats
350ml/12fl oz/1½ cups
  Almond Milk (page 20)
1 tsp brown sugar or coconut
  sugar
½ tsp ground cinnamon, plus
  extra to serve
a pinch of sea salt
1 banana, thinly sliced
250g/9oz strawberries, hulled
  and sliced
250g/9oz/1 cup dairy-free
  coconut yogurt
2 tbsp cacao nibs or vegan
  chocolate chips
carob powder, cocoa powder
  or raw cacao powder
  (optional), to serve

Put the oats in a medium saucepan and add the milk, 125ml/ 4fl oz/½ cup water, the sugar, cinnamon and salt.

Bring to a gentle boil over a medium heat, then reduce the heat to a simmer and cook for 10 minutes, stirring frequently. Add a little more water if the mixture is too thick. Cook for a further 5 minutes, or until thickened like porridge. Remove from the heat, then cool and chill in the fridge for 1 hour or overnight.

Spoon some oatmeal into two tall glasses, then add some banana slices, a few strawberry slices, and 1 tablespoon yogurt. Sprinkle with a few cacao nibs, then continue to layer until the glass is full. Top with any remaining strawberries and cacao nibs, dust with carob powder, if using, then serve. (Alternatively, make single layers, if you are using a larger glass.)

Soya-free   Seed-free

Gluten-free Soya-free

chia seed & coconut *pancakes*

Serves: 4
Preparation: 30 minutes,
**   plus 10 minutes soaking,**
**   plus making the spread**
Cooking: 20 minutes

½ tsp chia seeds
190g/6¾oz/1½ cups
    buckwheat flour
2 tsp gluten-free baking
    powder
875ml/30fl oz/3½ cups
    coconut milk
175g/6oz/½ cup Fruit &
    Pumpkin Spread (page 26),
    plus extra to serve
2 tbsp olive oil, safflower oil
    or coconut oil, plus extra
    if needed
desiccated coconut, berries,
    and agave syrup or brown
    rice syrup (optional),
    to serve

Preheat the oven to 100°C/200°F/Gas ½ and put a heatproof plate inside to warm. Put the chia seeds in a small bowl and add 3 tablespoons water. Leave to soak for 10 minutes to form a gel.

Sift the buckwheat flour and baking powder into a large mixing bowl and mix well.

In a separate bowl, whisk together the chia seed gel, coconut milk and the fruit spread. Add to the dry ingredients and stir gently to form a thick batter.

Heat 1½ teaspoons of the oil in a heavy-based frying pan over a medium heat. Pour 3–4 tablespoonfuls of batter into the pan, tilting the pan to cover the base of the pan with the mixture. Cook for 2–3 minutes on each side until lightly browned.

Repeat with the remaining batter, adding another 1½ teaspoons oil to the pan before cooking each one. Transfer the pancakes to the warmed plate, stacking them between sheets of baking parchment to prevent them from sticking together, and keep warm in the oven. Serve hot with a selection of toppings.

Banana makes this bread moist and flavoursome, and the peanuts add crunch and richness. You could also make the recipe using almond butter and even add some vegan chocolate chips.

peanut butter & banana bread

Makes: 1 loaf, 10 slices
Preparation: 15 minutes,
  plus making the milk
Cooking: 45 minutes, plus
  cooling

250g/9oz/2 cups plain flour
1½ tsp baking powder
1 vanilla pod
4 overripe bananas, cut into
  pieces
125ml/4fl oz/½ cup Almond
  Milk (page 20)
140g/5oz/½ cup sugar-free
  crunchy peanut butter
60ml/2fl oz/¼ cup safflower
  oil, sunflower oil or melted
  coconut oil
1 tsp ground cinnamon
80g/2¾oz/½ cup peanuts,
  roughly chopped

Preheat the oven to 180°C/350°F/Gas 4. Line the base and short sides of a non-stick 23 × 10cm/9 × 4in loaf tin with a strip of baking parchment and leave to one side. Sift the flour and baking powder into a large mixing bowl.

Split the vanilla pod in half lengthways and scrape out the seeds. Reserve the pod for another use. Put the bananas in a separate bowl and add the milk, vanilla seeds, peanut butter, oil and cinnamon. Using a hand blender, combine the ingredients until they form a smooth batter.

Pour this mixture into the dry ingredients and fold gently to combine. Spoon the mixture into the prepared loaf tin and spread out evenly. Sprinkle the peanuts over the top. Bake for 35–45 minutes until a skewer inserted into the centre comes out clean. Transfer to a wire rack and leave to cool in the tin before removing and serving. Store in an airtight container for up to 4 days.

Soya-free

Sugar-free

cinnamon *crumpets*

Makes: 6 crumpets
Preparation: 15 minutes, plus
 1 hour rising, and making
 the milk and optional butter
Cooking: 20 minutes

250g/9oz/2 cups plain flour
1 tsp ground cinnamon
½ tsp baking powder
a pinch of sea salt
7g/¼oz sachet (2¾ tsp) fast-
 action dried yeast
185ml/6fl oz/¾ cup Almond
 Milk (page 20), at room
 temperature
1 tbsp vegan margarine, plus
 extra for frying
Chocolate & Hazelnut Butter
 (page 26) and fresh fruit
 (optional), to serve

Sift the flour, cinnamon, baking powder and salt into a large bowl. Add the yeast, milk, margarine and 125ml/4fl oz/½ cup water, at room temperature. Whisk, or use a hand blender, to combine the mixture until smooth. Cover the bowl, and leave in a warm place for 1 hour, or until bubbles appear.

Put a small knob of margarine in a heavy-based, non-stick frying pan over a medium heat. Put two 10cm/4in non-stick metal food rings into the pan. Pour 4 tablespoonfuls of the batter into each ring. Cook over a medium heat for 3–4 minutes until the batter comes away from the rings – you will see it firming up on the side of the ring.

Remove the food rings carefully, using tongs, and turn the crumpets over using a palette knife. Cook the crumpets for a further 3–5 minutes until golden brown. (Alternatively, you can make the crumpets without the rings but they will be a pancake shape and will take less time to cook, 2–3 minutes on each side.) Wrap the crumpets in a clean tea towel and keep them warm, or serve them as you make them. Cook the remaining batter in the same way. Spread generously with the chocolate and hazelnut butter, and serve with some fresh fruit, if you like.

For extra protein you can add some silken tofu to this sustaining savoury breakfast a few minutes before it has finished cooking, if you like.

greek breakfast scramble

Serves: 2
Preparation: 15 minutes
Cooking: 50 minutes

4 medium potatoes, cut
  into cubes
1 tbsp olive oil or rice
  bran oil
1 large onion, finely chopped
juice of 1½ lemons
½ red pepper, deseeded and
  sliced
100g/3½oz button
  mushrooms, sliced
150g/5½oz/1 cup pitted
  Kalamata olives
1 small handful flat-leaf
  parsley leaves, torn
4 tbsp finely chopped basil
  leaves
1 tsp finely shredded mint
  leaves
sliced avocado and cherry
  tomatoes, to serve

Put the potato cubes in a saucepan, cover well with boiling water and cook for 5–8 minutes until just tender. Drain in a colander and leave to one side.

Heat the oil in a heavy-based frying pan over a medium heat. Add the onion, and cook for 10 minutes, or until translucent. Add the potatoes and lemon juice, and bring to a high simmer. Cook for 15 minutes, or until the lemon juice has reduced and the potatoes are golden brown.

Add the pepper, mushrooms and olives, and cook for 10 minutes. Remove from the heat and serve scattered with the parsley, basil and mint, and with the avocado slices and cherry tomatoes.

Gluten-free *Soya-free* *Nut-free* *Seed-free* *Sugar-free*

This versatile hash mixture can also be made into burgers or a rosti. Soak 1 tablespoon chia seeds in 3 tablespoons water for 10 minutes, then stir into the cooked hash. Form into burger shapes and fry in a little oil for 5 minutes.

sweet potato hash with tomato relish

Serves: 2 (with relish left over)
Preparation: 25 minutes
Cooking: 1 hour 10 minutes,
  plus cooling

1 tbsp olive oil or coconut oil
250g/9oz sweet potato,
  grated
1 large onion, chopped
60g/2¼oz kale, thinly sliced
1 tbsp lemon juice
chopped parsley leaves and
  diced avocado, to serve

TOMATO RELISH
4 medium tomatoes, chopped
1 large onion, chopped
1 red pepper, deseeded and
  cut into dice
1 tsp cider vinegar
2 tsp brown sugar or coconut
  sugar
1 tsp crushed chillies
350ml/12fl oz/1½ cups
  vegetable stock
sea salt and freshly ground
  black pepper

To make the relish, put all the ingredients in a large, heavy-based saucepan. Bring to a gentle boil over a medium heat, then reduce the heat to a low simmer and cook for 45 minutes, stirring frequently, or until the pepper is soft and the liquid has reduced. Adjust the seasoning to taste.

When the relish has thickened, remove the pan from the heat and leave to cool. Pour into a sterilized glass jar and store in the fridge for up to 4 weeks.

To make the hash, heat the oil in a heavy-based frying pan over a medium heat and add the sweet potato and onion. Season with salt and pepper. Cook for 10 minutes, stirring frequently, then add the kale and cook for a further 10 minutes, or until the sweet potato is crispy and the onion is soft. Drizzle over the lemon juice and sprinkle with parsley. Serve with diced avocado, and top with a large spoonful of tomato relish.

Gluten-free   Soya-free   Nut-free   Seed-free

This is a sublimely easy dish that is perfect for those days when you feel like being really lazy and having an effortless breakfast. Add the ingredients to a casserole, pop it in the oven and leave to cook – while tending to worldly matters – then come back later and enjoy! It can be prepared and cooked the night before, then reheated in the morning.

breakfast tagine

Serves: 2
Preparation: 20 minutes
Cooking: 1¼ hours

1 tbsp olive oil or coconut oil
1 large onion, sliced
2 garlic cloves, crushed
1 large aubergine, cut into cubes
2 courgettes, cut into dice
1 small red pepper, deseeded and thinly sliced
800g/1lb 12oz/3¼ cups tinned chopped tomatoes
1 tsp ground coriander
1 tsp paprika
1 tsp chilli powder
1 tsp ground cumin
½ tsp cumin seeds
½ tsp ground cinnamon
1 tsp sea salt
400g/14oz/1⅔ cups tinned butter beans, rinsed and drained
1 large avocado, cut in half, pitted, peeled and cut into dice
2 tsp chopped mint leaves
1 small handful of parsley leaves, chopped
sea salt and freshly ground black pepper
pitta bread, Chermoula Sauce (page 85) or hummus (optional), to serve

Preheat the oven to 200°C/400°F/Gas 6. Put the oil in a large casserole or baking dish with a lid, and add the onion, garlic, aubergine, courgettes and pepper.

Put the tomatoes in a bowl and add the coriander, paprika, chilli powder, ground cumin, cumin seeds, cinnamon and salt. Mix together well, then pour this mixture over the vegetables in the casserole and stir to combine. Add the butter beans and stir gently. Cover and cook in the oven for 45 minutes.

Take off the lid and check that the vegetables aren't sticking to the casserole. If necessary, add 60ml/2fl oz/¼ cup water. Season well with salt and pepper, then stir and cook for a further 15-30 minutes until the aubergine is soft. Scatter over the avocado and sprinkle with mint and parsley, then serve with the pitta bread and sauce.

 Gluten-free   Soya-free   Nut-free   Seed-free   Sugar-free

Gluten-free Nut-free Seed-free

vegie head *baked beans*

Serves: 4
Preparation: 10 minutes
Cooking: 25 minutes

1 tsp olive oil or coconut oil
1 onion, cut into dice
1 tsp mustard powder
1 tsp tomato purée
1 tsp tamari soy sauce, soy
  sauce or coconut aminos
1 tbsp brown sugar or
  coconut sugar
125ml/4fl oz/½ cup
  vegetable stock
250g/9oz/1 cup tinned
  chopped tomatoes
400g/14oz/1⅔ cups tinned
  butter beans or red kidney
  beans, rinsed and drained
sea salt and freshly ground
  black pepper
thickly sliced sourdough
  bread, fried spinach and
  mushrooms, to serve

Heat the oil in a large saucepan over a high heat and fry the onion for 5–8 minutes, stirring frequently, until softened.

Add the mustard powder, tomato purée, tamari and sugar, and stir to combine. Add the stock, tomatoes and beans. Bring to the boil over a medium-high heat, then cook for 10–15 minutes until the mixture thickens slightly and the beans are warmed through. Season with salt and pepper, and serve with bread, fried spinach and mushrooms.

Nut-free   Sugar-free

crêpes with spinach & *mushrooms*

Serves: 4
Preparation: 30 minutes,
  plus 1 hour resting
Cooking: 30 minutes

125ml/4fl oz/½ cup soya
  milk
50g/1¾oz/¼ cup vegan
  margarine
125g/4½oz/1 cup plain flour
1 tbsp olive oil or coconut oil
dairy-free yogurt and lemon
  wedges, to serve

SPINACH AND MUSHROOM
  FILLING
1 tsp olive oil or coconut oil
180g/6¼oz button
  mushrooms, thinly sliced
400g/14oz baby spinach
1 tbsp lemon juice
sea salt and freshly ground
  black pepper

Put the milk in a large bowl and add the margarine, flour and
a pinch of salt, then add 170ml/5½fl oz/⅔ cup water at room
temperature. Whisk, or use a hand blender, until smooth.
Cover the bowl with cling film, and put in the fridge for 1 hour.

Preheat the oven to 180°C/350°F/Gas 4 and put a heatproof
plate inside to warm. To cook the crêpes, heat 1 teaspoon of the
oil in an 18cm/7in frying pan and add just enough batter to coat
the base of the pan, tilting the pan to spread the mixture. Cook
until bubbles appear on the surface, then carefully turn the crêpe
over and cook on the other side until lightly golden. Put the
crêpe on to the warmed plate, then cover and keep warm in
the oven while you cook the remaining batter.

Meanwhile, to make the filling, heat the oil in a non-stick
saucepan over a low heat. Add the mushrooms and fry for
10 minutes, stirring frequently, or until the juices are released.
Add 1 teaspoon water at a time if the mushrooms begin to stick
to the pan. Add the spinach to the pan and reduce the heat to
low. Cook for 2–3 minutes until the spinach begins to wilt, then
stir in the lemon juice and season with salt and pepper.

Spoon 1 tablespoon of the filling on to one edge of a crêpe. Roll
it up gently. Continue with the remaining crêpes, then put the
filled crêpes in an ovenproof dish and reheat in the oven for
10 minutes. (Or serve them at room temperature, if you prefer.)
Serve with yogurt, and a lemon wedge.

Lunches

My favourite meal of the day is definitely lunch, because it gives me my biggest burst of energy – just right for a productive afternoon. I love to eat soups at any time of the year but particularly when the weather is colder, and the Mexican Bean Soup and Moroccan Quinoa Soup are hearty dishes for any season. There are salads to suit your mood and the weather. Some are fresh and raw, such as Courgette & Orange Carpaccio with Herbed Cheese, and others are griddled or roasted, such as Griddled Salad with Basil & Tahini Dressing or Roasted Pumpkin & Asparagus Salad. Many are suitable for making in advance and taking to work for maximum lunch envy, for picnics or when you're asked to 'bring along a plate'. My Sweet Potato Cups with Hummus & Walnut Pesto taste and look special and are a fun way to use tortilla wraps.

Sweet Potato Cups with
Hummus & Walnut Pesto
(page 86)

Traditional and modern Moroccan spices combine with cannellini beans and fibre- and protein-rich quinoa to make this soup a hearty meal. The soup can also be served with some crusty sourdough bread, a dollop of hummus and a squeeze of lemon, if you like.

moroccan quinoa soup

Serves: 4–6
Preparation: 15 minutes
Cooking: 35 minutes

2 tbsp olive oil or coconut oil
2 onions, finely chopped
3 garlic cloves, crushed
1 courgette, cut into dice
400g/14oz tomatoes, chopped
400g/14oz/2 cups tinned cannellini beans, drained and rinsed
1½ tbsp harissa paste
1 tsp turmeric
1 tsp ground cumin
1 tsp ground cinnamon
¼ tsp sweet paprika
200g/7oz/1 cup quinoa, rinsed and drained
2l/70fl oz/8 cups vegetable stock
80g/2¾oz kale, finely chopped
4 tbsp chopped mint leaves
sea salt and freshly ground black pepper
dairy-free yogurt, to serve

Heat the oil in a large, heavy-based saucepan over a medium heat. Add the onions and garlic, and cook for 5–8 minutes until softened.

Add the courgette, tomatoes, beans, harissa, spices, quinoa and stock, then season and stir well. Bring to the boil over a high heat, then reduce the heat to medium-high and cook for 15 minutes, stirring frequently, or until the quinoa is tender and translucent.

Add the kale and cook for a further 5 minutes, then remove from the heat. Sprinkle over the mint leaves and serve with a large spoonful of yogurt.

Gluten-free Soya-free Nut-free Seed-free Sugar-free

Sweet, smoky chillies and a hint of paprika give this soup the aroma and flavour that remind me of eating true Mexican food in America. I'm immediately transported to the small, wooden building with sombreros hanging on the walls, neon signs promoting *cerveza* (beer) – and amazing traditional food.

mexican bean soup

Serves: 6
Preparation: 20 minutes
Cooking: 40 minutes

2 tbsp olive oil or coconut oil
2 onions, chopped
3 garlic cloves, crushed
350g/12oz tomatoes, chopped
500ml/17fl oz/2 cups vegetable stock
400g/14oz/2 cups tinned red kidney beans, rinsed and drained
1 tsp smoked paprika
1 tsp sea salt
1 tsp dried oregano
1 tbsp dried ancho chillies, or 1 tsp ancho or regular chilli powder
200g/7oz/1 cup tinned black beans, rinsed and drained

TO SERVE
vegan soured cream or dairy-free yogurt
diced avocado
lime wedges
crushed corn chips
finely sliced red chillies
coriander leaves

Heat the oil in a large, heavy-based saucepan over a medium heat. Add the onions and garlic, and cook for 10 minutes, or until translucent. Add the tomatoes, stock, kidney beans, paprika, salt, oregano and chillies, and return to the boil, then simmer for 5 minutes.

Using a hand blender, process the mixture until smooth, then add the black beans and cook for a further 15 minutes, or until the liquid has reduced and the black beans are thoroughly heated through. Serve with a dollop of soured cream and top with diced avocado, a squeeze of lime juice and a sprinkle of corn chips, red chillies and coriander.

 Gluten-free *Soya-free* *Nut-free* *Seed-free* *Sugar-free*

Here is a traditional hot-and-sour Indian soup with herbs and spices melding together to create an authentic flavour. If you prefer your soup a little thicker, use less water or add some leftover cooked brown rice or quinoa.

rasam *soup*

Serves: 4
Preparation: 15 minutes
Cooking: 30 minutes

220g/7¾oz/1 cup red lentils, rinsed and drained
400g/14oz/scant 1⅔ cups tinned chopped tomatoes
2l/70fl oz/8 cups vegetable stock
1 tsp olive oil or coconut oil
1 tsp cumin seeds
1 tsp mustard seeds
8 garlic cloves, crushed
1 large onion, finely chopped
1cm/½in piece fresh root ginger, peeled and grated
½ tsp ground turmeric
½ tsp ground coriander
1 dried red chilli or ½ tsp crushed chillies, or to taste
2 tsp tamarind paste
juice of 2 lemons
juice of 1 lime
1 large handful of coriander leaves, chopped

Put the lentils in a large, heavy-based saucepan and add the tomatoes and stock. Bring to the boil over a high heat, then lower the heat to medium-high and cook for 20 minutes, or until the lentils are soft.

Meanwhile, heat the oil in a non-stick frying pan over a medium heat. Add the cumin and mustard seeds to the pan, and stir-fry for 30 seconds, or until the seeds begin to pop. Add the garlic and onion to the frying pan and cook for 10 minutes, or until the onion is translucent.

Using a hand blender, process the lentil mixture until smooth. Return to a low heat to keep warm.

Stir the ginger into the frying pan and add the turmeric, ground coriander and dried chilli, then fry for 30 seconds, or until fragrant. Add the spicy onion to the blended lentils and stir in the tamarind paste, lemon juice and lime juice. Stir in the fresh coriander and serve.

Gluten-free   Soya-free   Nut-free   Seed-free   Sugar-free

One weekend away some years ago I was treated to dinner at a fine-dining restaurant where we were served little shot glasses filled with a bright yellow soup – it was a cream of corn and lemongrass. As I sipped it, it was like a thousand fireworks going off inside my mouth. If I close my eyes, I can still remember the experience. I came home and created my own, healthier version. Serve this in bowls for lunch or in shot glasses for a flavour explosion to start a main meal.

thai sweetcorn soup

Serves: 4
Preparation: 5 minutes,
** plus making the crisps**
Cooking: 35 minutes

1 tbsp olive oil or coconut oil
1 small leek, white part only, thinly sliced
1 lemongrass stalk, outer leaves removed, white part sliced
1 small red chilli, deseeded and sliced (optional)
500ml/17fl oz/2 cups coconut cream
300g/10½oz/2 cups fresh or frozen sweetcorn
750ml/26fl oz/3 cups vegetable stock
½ tsp brown sugar or coconut sugar
juice of 1 lime
2 kaffir lime leaves, torn
sea salt
Baked Chilli Vegetable Crisps (page 96) to serve

Heat the oil in a heavy-based saucepan over a medium heat, and add the leek, lemongrass and chilli. Cook for 5–6 minutes until the leek is tender.

Add the coconut cream, sweetcorn, stock, sugar, lime juice and salt to taste, and bring to the boil. Lower the heat, and simmer for 15 minutes. Using a blender or food processor, process the ingredients until smooth and silky. Add the kaffir lime leaves and simmer for a further 2 minutes, then serve with the vegetable crisps.

Gluten-free   *Soya-free*   *Seed-free*

kale & soba noodles with
ginger - chilli sauce

Serves: 4
Preparation: 15 minutes
Cooking: 20 minutes

350g/12oz dried soba
  noodles
1 tsp olive oil or coconut oil
200g/7oz smoked tofu, cut
  into cubes
3 carrots, cut into matchstick
  strips
1 large red onion, sliced
200g/7oz button mushrooms,
  sliced
50g/1¾oz red cabbage,
  thinly sliced
80g/2¾oz kale, sliced

GINGER–CHILLI SAUCE
1 garlic clove, crushed
2 tbsp soy sauce or tamari
  soy sauce
2 tbsp toasted sesame oil
2cm/¾in piece fresh root
  ginger, peeled and grated
juice of 1 lime
1 tsp chilli paste
1 tsp brown sugar or coconut
  sugar

Put all the sauce ingredients in a small bowl and add 125ml/
4fl oz/½ cup water. Whisk well to combine thoroughly, then
leave to one side to allow the flavours to develop.

Bring a large saucepan of water to the boil over a high heat, and
cook the soba noodles for 4–5 minutes, or according to the pack
instructions, until soft. Drain in a colander and leave to one side.

Heat the oil in a large wok or non-stick saucepan over a high
heat. Fry the tofu for 5 minutes, turning frequently, until golden
brown on all sides. Add the carrots, onion and mushrooms, and
stir-fry for 1 minute, or until warmed through. Add the cabbage
and kale, and cook for 2 minutes, or until they begin to soften.
Pour the sauce mixture over the top and cook for a further
3 minutes, stirring frequently. Add the soba noodles and stir to
combine. Cook for 1 minute, or until thoroughly heated through.
Remove from the heat and serve immediately.

In the middle of winter, I crave this rustic soup, with its earthy flavours from the root vegetables and brown lentils and a kick from red chilli. Any leftovers are perfect reheated for lunch the next day.

winter lentil soup

Serves: 6
Preparation: 15 minutes
Cooking: 55 minutes

6 ripe tomatoes
1 tbsp olive oil or
   safflower oil
2 large onions, chopped
4 large garlic cloves, crushed
1 large potato, cut into cubes
2 carrots, sliced
3 celery sticks, sliced
500g/1lb 2oz/2¾ cups dried
   brown or green lentils,
   rinsed and drained
2l/70fl oz/8 cups vegetable
   stock
1 bay leaf
1 red chilli, deseeded and
   sliced
1 handful of parsley leaves
sea salt and freshly ground
   black pepper

Plunge the tomatoes into boiling water for 30 seconds, then refresh in a bowl of cold water. Peel away the skins and roughly chop the flesh. Leave to one side. Heat the oil in a large saucepan over a medium heat and fry the onions for 10 minutes, or until translucent. Add the garlic and cook for a further 2 minutes.

Add the potato, carrots and celery, and stir-fry for 3 minutes, or until sizzling. Add the lentils, tomatoes, stock and the bay leaf and chilli. Season well with salt and pepper. Bring to the boil over a high heat, then reduce the heat to medium-high and cook for 25 minutes, or until the lentils are soft. Serve sprinkled with the parsley.

Gluten-free   *Soya-free*   *Nut-free*   *Seed-free*   *Sugar-free*

My tahini dressing with a citrussy zing and the sweetness of basil lifts the flavours of griddled vegetables and makes a rich and satisfying lunch. The dressing also tastes good with falafels or as a dip.

griddled salad with basil & *tahini dressing*

Serves: 4
Preparation: 30 minutes
Cooking: 40 minutes

4 large courgettes, thinly
  sliced lengthways
2 aubergines, thinly sliced
  lengthways
1 fennel bulb, cut into
  quarters and thickly sliced
1 small head of cauliflower,
  thickly sliced
4 large portobello
  mushrooms, thinly sliced
1 tbsp olive oil or melted
  coconut oil
4 large handfuls of mixed
  salad leaves, such as
  dandelion, mint, parsley,
  coriander, mustard, beetroot
  greens, rocket and kale,
  to serve

TAHINI DRESSING
60g/2¼oz/¼ cup tahini
250ml/9fl oz/1 cup orange
  juice
zest and juice of ½ lemon
2 garlic cloves, crushed
¼ tsp.ground sea salt
1 small handful of basil
  leaves

Preheat the oven to 100°C/200°F/Gas ½ and put a plate inside to warm. Heat a large, ridged griddle over a medium-high heat. Put all the vegetables in a large bowl and add the oil, then toss gently to coat the vegetables and tip into the griddle. You may need to cook these in batches. Spread the vegetables out evenly. Cook for 8–10 minutes until marked with golden lines on one side. Reduce the heat, if necessary, to avoid burning.

Meanwhile, make the dressing. Put all the ingredients into a blender or food processor, then process on high speed for 30 seconds, or until the dressing is smooth and creamy. Leave to one side to allow the flavours to develop.

Turn the vegetables over and cook for 8 minutes, or until there are golden lines on the second side. Transfer the cooked vegetables to the warm plate while you cook the remaining batches. Put the salad leaves on a large serving plate and put the cooked vegetables on top, then drizzle with the tahini dressing. Serve immediately.

Gluten-free *Soya-free* *Nut-free* *Sugar-free*

The sweetness of the tomatoes complements the nutty flavour of the chickpeas and the freshness of the mint. If you like, substitute some of the cherry tomatoes with yellow plum tomatoes to add a beautiful contrast.

chickpea, mint & tomato salad

Serves: 4
Preparation: 10 minutes

800g/1lb 12oz/scant 4 cups tinned chickpeas, drained and rinsed
1 garlic clove, crushed
½ red onion, finely sliced
2 spring onions, finely sliced
½ yellow pepper, deseeded and thinly sliced
1 small handful of mint leaves, chopped or left whole
20 cherry tomatoes, or baby plum tomatoes, cut in half
2 tbsp extra virgin olive oil
1 tsp cider vinegar
½ tsp wholegrain mustard
sea salt and freshly ground black pepper

Put the chickpeas in a large serving bowl and add the garlic, red onion, spring onions, pepper, mint and tomatoes.

Pour the olive oil into a small bowl and add the vinegar and mustard. Whisk well, then drizzle over the salad. Season with salt and pepper, and serve immediately. Store in an airtight container in the fridge for up to 3 days.

Gluten-free *Soya-free* *Nut-free* *Seed-free* *Sugar-free*

Containing fibre, protein and a large dose of antioxidants, this salad is colourful and surprisingly filling. It's perfect to take to work, on picnics, for barbecues and even for the kids' school lunches. Any beetroot will work well with this salad, but if you can find one of the more unusual beetroots, such as this pink and white salad variety, it will make the dish look particularly attractive.

sweet *super-food salad*

Serves 6
Preparation: 20 minutes

100g/3½oz mixed baby salad leaves
300g/10½oz/2 cups cherry tomatoes, cut in half
200g/7oz strawberries, sliced
2 beetroot, thinly sliced or grated
30g/1oz/1 cup alfalfa sprouts
2 large cucumbers, thinly sliced
2 avocados, cut in half, peeled, pitted and sliced
1 tbsp chia seeds
150g/5½oz/heaped 1 cup hazelnuts, roughly chopped
1 tbsp sunflower seeds
1 tbsp pumpkin seeds

DRESSING
1 tbsp lemon juice
2 tbsp cider vinegar
60ml/2fl oz/¼ cup extra virgin olive oil
2 tsp wholegrain mustard
sea salt and freshly ground black pepper

To make the dressing, put all the ingredients in a screwtop jar, cover and shake well to combine. (Alternatively, whisk in a small jug.) Leave to one side to allow the flavours to develop.

Put all the salad ingredients in a large serving bowl, and toss gently to combine. Drizzle with the dressing, then toss and serve immediately.

 Gluten-free Soya-free Sugar-free Raw

Gluten-free   Soya-free   Seed-free

roasted pumpkin &
asparagus salad

Serves: 4
Preparation: 15 minutes
Cooking: 25 minutes

12 asparagus spears
550g/1lb 4oz pumpkin or
  butternut squash, peeled
  and sliced into half-moons
3 garlic cloves, crushed
2 tbsp olive oil or melted
  coconut oil
250g/9oz cherry tomatoes
100g/3½oz/1 cup mixed
  nuts, roughly chopped
sea salt and freshly ground
  black pepper

MUSTARD DRESSING
4 tbsp olive oil or melted
  coconut oil
2 tsp brown sugar, brown rice
  syrup or agave syrup
1 tsp wholegrain mustard
½ tsp sea salt

Snap off any woody ends from the asparagus stalks at the point where they break easily, then cut the tender spears into 1cm/½in pieces if large, otherwise leave whole. Leave to one side. Preheat the oven to 220°C/425°F/Gas 7.

Put the pumpkin and garlic on a baking tray and season well with salt and pepper. Add 1 tablespoon of the oil and toss to combine, then spread the mixture in the tray evenly. Roast for 15 minutes. Add the cherry tomatoes and asparagus, brush with the remaining oil, then season and bake for a further 10 minutes, or until tender.

Meanwhile, to make the dressing, put the oil in a small bowl and add the sugar, mustard and salt, then whisk together. Remove the vegetables from the oven and leave to one side to cool slightly. Toss the warm vegetables with the dressing and top with the nuts, then serve.

The sweet orange and the herby saltiness of the cheese are matched perfectly with the courgette in this simple and fresh-tasting dish. You could also add some grated beetroot or fried tempeh to make it more substantial.

courgette & orange carpaccio
with herbed cheese

Serves: 4
Preparation: 15 minutes,
  plus making the cheese

2 oranges
2 tbsp good-quality extra
  virgin olive oil
1 tbsp lemon juice
450g/1lb courgettes,
  preferably a mixture of
  green and yellow, thinly
  sliced
¼ quantity Herbed Almond
  Cheese (page 22), crumbled
4 tbsp mint leaves, finely
  sliced or left whole
4 tbsp basil leaves, finely
  sliced or left whole
sea salt and freshly ground
  black pepper

Using a sharp knife, cut a thin slice of peel and pith from each end of an orange. Put the orange cut-side down on a plate and cut off the peel and pith in strips. Remove any remaining pith. Cut out each segment, leaving the membrane behind. Leave to one side. Squeeze the remaining juice from the membrane into a small bowl. Repeat with the second orange.

Pour the olive oil into the bowl with the orange juice and add the lemon juice and a pinch of salt. Arrange the courgette slices and orange segments on a serving plate, overlapping them slightly. Add the herbed cheese and sprinkle with the herbs. Drizzle with the dressing, grind over some pepper and serve.

Gluten-free *Soya-free* *Seed-free* *Sugar-free* *Raw*

I made this salad for one of my clients who has to follow a very limited diet. It just goes to show that even the most simple of ingredients can be turned into something enticing. The salad can be served warm, as here, or cold.

noodle, courgette &
avocado salad

Serves: 4
Preparation: 15 minutes
Cooking: 5 minutes

350g/12oz brown rice
  noodles
2 courgettes, thinly sliced
1 tbsp black sesame seeds
  and mixed baby salad
  leaves, to serve

AVOCADO DRESSING
2 avocados, cut in half,
  peeled and pitted
250ml/9fl oz/1 cup coconut
  milk
2 handfuls of basil leaves
1 tsp sea salt
2 tbsp toasted sesame oil
2 tsp mirin or rice wine
2 tsp white wine vinegar

Bring a large saucepan of water to the boil over a high heat. Add the rice noodles and courgette slices, then reduce the heat to medium and cook for 2 minutes. Drain in a colander and rinse under cold water, then leave to one side to cool.

To make the dressing, put the avocados into a blender or food processor and add the coconut milk, basil, salt, oil, mirin and vinegar. Blend until smooth.

Tip the drained noodles and courgettes back into the pan and add the dressing. Toss until coated in the dressing. Sprinkle with sesame seeds and serve immediately with the salad leaves.

Gluten-free   *Soya-free*   *Sugar-free*

curried chickpea patties with satay dipping sauce

Serves: 4
Preparation: 20 minutes
Cooking: 1 hour, plus cooling

60g/2¼oz/⅓ cup brown rice
400g/14oz/2 cups tinned
   chickpeas, rinsed and
   drained
100ml/3½fl oz/⅓ cup
   coconut milk
½ tsp brown sugar or
   coconut sugar
70g/2½oz/⅔ cup fresh
   breadcrumbs
1 tsp mild curry powder
½ tsp cumin seeds
½ tsp onion powder
1 tsp sea salt
2 tbsp olive oil or coconut oil
green salad, to serve

SATAY DIPPING SAUCE
160g/5¾oz/1 cup unsalted
   dry-roasted peanuts
80ml/2½fl oz/⅓ cup coconut
   milk
1 garlic clove
½ tsp soy sauce, tamari soy
   sauce or coconut aminos
1 tbsp toasted sesame oil
2 tsp brown sugar or
   coconut sugar
½ tsp tamarind paste
2 tsp crushed chillies

Bring a large saucepan of water to the boil over a high heat. Add the rice and cook for 35–40 minutes, or according to the pack instructions, until tender. Drain in a colander and leave to one side to cool.

Meanwhile, to make the satay sauce, put the peanuts into a food processor and process into a fine paste, then add the remaining sauce ingredients and 80ml/2½fl oz/⅓ cup water. Process until smooth and combined, then leave to one side.

Put the chickpeas into a blender or food processor and pulse until chopped. Add the coconut milk, sugar, breadcrumbs, curry powder, cumin seeds, onion powder, salt and rice, then blend to combine. Heat 1 tablespoon of the oil in a non-stick frying pan over a medium heat.

Using a spoon, scoop out golf-ball-sized pieces of mixture and form into little patties. Fry in the oil for 3–4 minutes until golden on one side. You will probably have to do this in batches. Turn the patties over and cook for 2 minutes on the other side. Remove from the pan and keep warm. Continue until all the mixture is cooked, adding more oil as necessary. Serve with the dipping sauce and green salad.

The trick to making easy rolls is to have everything cut up and ready to assemble, then it takes moments to complete.

rice paper & nori rolls

Serves: 4
Preparation: 25 minutes,
  plus 2 minutes soaking

50g/1¾oz rice noodles
8 rice paper sheets
2 carrots, cut into
  matchstick strips
1 cucumber, cut into
  matchstick strips
½ red pepper, deseeded and
  cut into matchstick strips
80g/2¾oz/½ cup almonds,
  finely chopped
1 tbsp chia seeds
1 handful of mint leaves,
  finely chopped
1 handful of coriander leaves,
  finely chopped
2 nori sheets, cut into
  quarters

SESAME DIPPING SAUCE
4 tbsp tamari soy sauce or
  coconut aminos
½ spring onion, finely sliced
1 tsp mirin or rice wine
  vinegar
2 tsp toasted sesame oil
1 tsp brown sugar or
  coconut sugar
1 tsp crushed chillies
1 tsp sesame seeds

To make the sauce, put all the ingredients in a bowl and whisk together. Leave to one side to allow the flavours to develop.

Put the rice noodles in a saucepan and pour over boiling water to cover generously. Leave to soak for 2 minutes, then drain thoroughly in a colander.

Pour boiling water into a large heatproof bowl or saucepan to a depth of 1cm/½in. Submerge a rice paper sheet for 10–15 seconds until it becomes transparent and flimsy. Carefully lift it out and lay it flat on a plate, then fill it as follows.

Starting close to the edge of the rice paper nearest to you, start to make a narrow layer of filling along that horizontal edge, using a one-eighth portion of rice noodles. Now layer a one-eighth portion of carrot, cucumber, pepper, almonds, chia seeds, mint and coriander on top. Pick up the lower edge of the rice paper and tuck it over the filling, then, using flat hands, make one rolling movement to cover the filling in some of the rice paper. Tuck in the sides and roll again tightly to finish.

Put the rice paper roll on one quarter of a nori sheet and roll it up in the nori sheet. Leave to one side and repeat with the remaining rice paper sheets. Cut each roll in half and serve with the dipping sauce.

Gluten-free

Nut-free

tempura pumpkin stacks with ginger dressing

Serves: 4
Preparation: 30 minutes
Cooking: 25 minutes

safflower oil or sunflower oil,
 for deep-frying
210g/7½oz/1¾ cups plain
 flour
60g/2¼oz/½ cup cornflour
1 tsp baking powder
a pinch of sea salt
¼ tsp mustard powder
2 tsp white sesame seeds
2 tsp black sesame seeds
1kg/2lb 4oz pumpkin or
 butternut squash, peeled,
 deseeded, and sliced into
 half-rounds 3mm/⅛in thick
200g/7oz salad leaves
Tamari Spiced Nuts &
 Seeds (page 94), to serve
 (optional)

GINGER DRESSING
1 tsp sesame oil
1cm/½in piece fresh root
 ginger, peeled and grated
1 tbsp soy sauce or tamari
 soy sauce
1 tsp brown rice syrup, agave
 syrup or brown sugar
juice of ½ lemon
juice of 1 lime
1 spring onion, white part
 only, finely sliced

Preheat the oven to 100°C/200°F/Gas ½. Put a wire rack on to a baking sheet and put inside the oven to warm. Put all the ingredients for the dressing in a screwtop jar, cover and shake well to combine. (Alternatively, whisk in a small jug.) Leave to one side to allow the flavours to develop.

Heat a wok, a large saucepan or a deep-fryer with the oil for deep-frying to 170°C (test by frying a small cube of bread – it should brown in 40 seconds). Sift 125g/4½oz/1 cup of the flour with the cornflour, baking powder, salt and mustard into a large bowl. Slowly pour in 455ml/16fl oz/scant 2 cups water and whisk together until smooth. The mixture should be the consistency of double cream.

Put all the sesame seeds in a non-stick frying pan and dry-fry over a low heat for 30 seconds, shaking the pan constantly, until just beginning to brown. Remove from the heat and set aside.

Dust each pumpkin piece with the remaining flour, and then dip it into the batter to coat well, dipping a few times if necessary. Put some pumpkin pieces into the hot oil and leave to fry for 4 minutes or until lightly golden. Lift out with a slotted spoon. Arrange on the wire rack and put into the oven while you fry the remaining pumpkin. Layer the pumpkin slices over the salad leaves and sprinkle with the sesame seeds and spiced nuts and seeds, if you like. Serve drizzled with the dressing.

Nut-free

chinese spring onion pancakes with *dipping sauce*

Serves: 4
Preparation: 20 minutes,
plus 30 minutes resting
Cooking: 15 minutes

7g/¼oz sachet (2¾ tsp) fast-action dried yeast
a pinch of sugar
125g/4½oz/1 cup plain flour, plus extra for dusting
75g/2½oz/½ cup wholemeal flour
3 tbsp safflower oil or sunflower oil, plus extra for greasing
2 tbsp toasted sesame oil
4 spring onions, finely chopped

GINGER DIPPING SAUCE
3 tbsp soy sauce or tamari soy sauce
1 tbsp white wine vinegar
1 tsp mirin
1 tsp chilli oil
2 tsp toasted sesame oil
½ tsp brown sugar or coconut sugar, or brown rice syrup or agave syrup
1 garlic clove, crushed
5mm/¼in fresh root ginger, peeled and grated
1 spring onion, thinly sliced

To make the dipping sauce, put all the ingredients in a small serving bowl and whisk together. Leave to one side for the flavours to develop. Put the yeast in a small bowl, and add 125ml/4fl oz/½ cup warm water and the sugar, then whisk together. Sift the flours into a large bowl, and tip in any bran remaining in the sieve. Stir in the yeast mixture, then use your hands to incorporate all the flour into the liquid. (Alternatively, sift the flours into a food processor. With the blades turning, slowly pour in the yeast mixture, until the mixture forms a dough.)

Turn the dough on to a lightly floured surface and knead for 2–4 minutes until smooth. (Or, if your machine has a kneading function, set this for 1 minute.) Lightly oil a large bowl, add the dough and cover with a damp tea towel. Leave in a warm place for 30 minutes.

Divide the dough into 20 pieces, roll them into balls, then put them on a floured surface and roll them flat. Brush some sesame oil over each one, and sprinkle with the spring onions. Roll the dough circles into a cigar shape, then roll them up again from one end to the other, to make a spiral. With the spiral laying flat, roll the dough into a thin circle. Heat the safflower oil in a large frying pan and fry the pancakes for 2–3 minutes on each side. Serve with the dipping sauce.

Soya-free Nut-free Seed-free Sugar-free

lemon, artichoke & baby spinach spaghetti

Serves: 4
Preparation: 10 minutes
Cooking: 15 minutes

350g/12oz wholewheat
  spaghetti
175g/6oz bottled or tinned
  marinated artichoke hearts,
  drained and cut into
  quarters
juice of 2 lemons
2 tsp finely grated lemon zest
2 large handfuls of basil
  leaves
50g/1¾oz baby spinach
  leaves
extra virgin olive oil, to
  drizzle
sea salt and freshly ground
  black pepper

Bring a large saucepan of salted water to the boil over a high heat, add the spaghetti and cook for 10-12 minutes, or according to the pack instructions, until just tender. Drain the spaghetti in a colander, reserving 4 tablespoons of the cooking liquid, and return both the pasta and the reserved water to the pan.

Add the artichoke hearts, lemon juice and zest, basil and spinach to the pan and mix well.

Drizzle the olive oil over the pasta to taste and serve with plenty of black pepper.

moroccan stuffed mushrooms

Serves: 4
Preparation: 20 minutes
Cooking: 45 minutes

200g/7oz/1 cup quinoa,
  rinsed and drained
2 tsp tamari soy sauce or soy
  sauce, or to taste
8 large portobello
  mushrooms, stems
  separated and finely
  chopped
800g/1lb 12oz/3¼ cups
  tinned chopped tomatoes
4 garlic cloves, crushed
230g/8oz courgettes, finely
  chopped
1 tsp chermoula paste or
  chilli powder, or to taste
4 tbsp chopped basil leaves
2 tsp sweet paprika
1 tsp ground turmeric
½ tsp ground cinnamon
sea salt and freshly ground
  black pepper
salad leaves, to serve

CHERMOULA SAUCE
1 large handful of coriander
  leaves
2 large handfuls of parsley
  leaves
4 garlic cloves
½ tsp sea salt
2 tsp ground cumin
1 tsp sweet paprika
¼ tsp crushed chillies
2 saffron threads
80ml/2½fl oz/⅓ cup extra
  virgin olive oil
juice of 1 large lemon

Preheat the oven to 180°C/350°F/Gas 4, and line a baking tray with baking parchment. Put the quinoa in a pan and add 250ml/9fl oz/1 cup water. Bring to the boil over a high heat, then reduce the heat to medium-low and simmer for 15 minutes, or until tender and translucent, and the water has mostly been absorbed. Drain in a sieve, then tip back into the pan. Season to taste with pepper and tamari.

Meanwhile, put the mushroom caps on the prepared baking tray, then leave to one side.

Put the tomatoes in a saucepan over a medium heat and add the garlic, courgettes, chermoula paste, chopped mushroom stems, basil, paprika, turmeric and cinnamon. Bring to the boil and then reduce the heat to a simmer. Season with salt and pepper. Cook for 10 minutes, stirring frequently, then remove from the heat.

Meanwhile, put all the chermoula sauce ingredients into a blender or food processor and blend until smooth.

Spoon an eighth of the quinoa into each mushroom, and top with the tomato mixture. Cook the mushrooms in the oven for 15 minutes and serve with the salad leaves and a spoonful of the chermoula sauce.

 Gluten-free   Nut-free   Seed-free   Sugar-free

Soya-free   *Sugar-free*

sweet potato cups with hummus & walnut pesto

Serves: 3–6
Preparation: 30 minutes,
   plus cooling and making
   the hummus
Cooking: 1 hour

250g/9oz sweet potato, cut
   into small dice
1 tbsp olive oil or coconut oil,
   plus extra for greasing
½ courgette, cut into small
   dice
3 flour tortillas
1 large handful of basil leaves
1 small handful of parsley
   leaves
100g/3½oz baby spinach
   leaves
30g/1oz/¼ cup walnuts
60ml/2fl oz/¼ cup good-
   quality extra virgin olive oil
1 garlic clove, crushed
a squeeze of lemon juice, or
   to taste
sea salt and freshly ground
   black pepper
220g/7¾oz/1 cup hummus,
   such as Roasted Garlic
   & Hazelnut Hummus
   (page 98)

Preheat the oven to 200°C/400°F/Gas 6. Put the sweet potato in a bowl and add the oil. Mix well to coat thoroughly and tip on to a baking tray. Roast for 30 minutes, then add the courgette to the tray. Roast for a further 15 minutes, or until tender.

While the vegetables are cooking, cut each tortilla into quarters and, using a small amount of oil, grease six muffin cups. Press 1 piece of tortilla inside a muffin cup and smooth into the edges to line the cup, then add a second piece at an angle and smooth in the same way. Leave the edges overhanging, to create a tortilla 'cup'. Leave to one side.

Put the basil into a blender or food processor and add the parsley and spinach leaves, then process until they are well combined. Add the walnuts, olive oil, garlic and lemon juice. Season with salt and pepper, and blend into a smooth paste to make a pesto.

When the sweet potato is cooked, leave the baking tray on one side to cool. When the vegetables are cool, tip them into a large mixing bowl, and combine with 2 tablespoons of walnut pesto. Spoon the sweet potato and courgette mixture into each tortilla cup and bake for 15 minutes, or until the tortillas are golden brown. Top with a large spoonful of hummus and serve with the remaining pesto. The pesto can be stored in a sterilized jar in the fridge for up to 1 week or frozen for up to 1 month.

This simple curry can be changed in many ways to suit what you have in your storecupboard or for a different flavour emphasis. You can add potatoes, red kidney beans, spinach, kale or pumpkin or you can increase the chilli and garam masala, or try some lime juice and a dash of coconut cream.

super - fast chickpea curry

Serves: 4
Preparation: 15 minutes,
** plus making the parathas**
Cooking: 30 minutes

1 tbsp olive oil or coconut oil
2 onions, finely chopped
3 garlic cloves, crushed
5mm/¼in piece fresh root
  ginger, peeled and grated
1 tsp yellow mustard seeds
1 tsp cumin seeds
1½ tsp garam masala
1 tsp ground turmeric
1 tsp ground cumin
2 tsp dried fenugreek leaves
  or 1 tsp dried fenugreek
400g/14oz/scant 1⅔ cups
  tinned chopped tomatoes
1 large tomato, chopped
800g/1lb 12oz/scant 4 cups
  tinned chickpeas, rinsed
  and drained
1 tsp crushed chillies, or to
  taste (optional)
2 tbsp chopped coriander
  leaves
sea salt
Garlic Parathas (page 27),
  to serve

Heat the oil in a large, heavy-based saucepan over a medium heat. Add the onions, garlic and ginger, and cook for 5–8 minutes until softened. Add 1 teaspoon of water if the onions start to catch on the base of the pan.

Move the cooked onions to one side of the pan, and add the mustard seeds and cumin seeds to the other side. Leave them for a few seconds, then start to move them with a spoon and stir-fry for 30 seconds, or until they begin to pop. Stir them into the onions and add 2 teaspoons water. Add the garam masala, turmeric, ground cumin and fenugreek, and stir well. The mixture will become a thick, brown paste.

Add the tinned and fresh tomatoes, the chickpeas and 500ml/17fl oz/2 cups water. Stir well and bring to the boil, then reduce the heat and simmer over a medium-high heat for 15 minutes. Season with salt and add the crushed chillies, if using. Scatter over the coriander and serve with the parathas.

Gluten-free   *Soya-free*   *Nut-free*   *Seed-free*   *Sugar-free*

Sugar-free

creamy bean *quesadillas*

Serves: 4
Preparation: 15 minutes,
plus making the sauce
Cooking: 10 minutes

400g/14oz/2 cups tinned
  red kidney beans, rinsed
  and drained
1 tsp ground cumin
¼ tsp ground cinnamon
3 tbsp tahini
1 tsp paprika
1 tsp crushed chillies
3 garlic cloves
1 avocado
8 wholemeal or plain flour
  tortillas
1 quantity Vegan Cheese
  Sauce (page 23)
115g/4oz/½ cup mild salsa,
  plus extra to serve
1 large handful of coriander
  leaves
50g/1¾oz red cabbage, very
  thinly sliced
1 small handful of baby
  spinach leaves, torn
1 red onion, very thinly sliced

Put the kidney beans into a food processor and add the cumin, cinnamon, tahini, paprika, crushed chillies and garlic. Blend until smooth.

Cut the avocado in half, remove the pit and peel, then cut into chunks and put into a small bowl. Roughly mash with a fork.

Heat a large, non-stick frying pan over a medium heat. Lay 4 tortillas on the work surface. Spread a layer of the kidney bean mixture over each tortilla, then add a large spoonful of the vegan cheese sauce.

Spoon the avocado over the tortillas and top with some salsa, coriander leaves, red cabbage, spinach and slices of red onion. Put a tortilla on top of each to make quesadillas. Put 1 quesadilla into the frying pan. Dry-fry on each side for 1 minute, or until golden brown. Repeat with the remaining quesadillas. Serve with the remaining sauce and the salsa.

Gluten-free *Nut-free* *Sugar-free*

mushroom & roasted beetroot *polenta nests*

Serves: 6
Preparation: 20 minutes,
  plus 1 hour chilling
Cooking: 1½ hours,
  plus cooling

2 tbsp olive oil, plus extra
  for greasing
625ml/21⅛fl oz/2½ cups
  boiling vegetable stock, or
  according to the polenta
  pack instructions
220g/7¾oz/1½ cups fine
  polenta
2 tsp crushed chillies
2 large beetroots, cut into
  quarters
1 garlic clove
2 tbsp lemon juice
1 tsp ground cumin
1 tbsp vegan cream cheese
1 tsp safflower oil or
  sunflower oil
600g/1lb 5oz mixed
  mushrooms, such as
  button, chestnut, shiitake
  and enoki, sliced
sea salt and freshly ground
  black pepper
green salad, to serve

Preheat the oven to 180°C/350°F/Gas 4 and lightly grease six non-stick individual tart tins. Pour the boiling stock into a medium saucepan, return to the boil, and add 1 teaspoon salt. Pour in the polenta in a fine stream, whisking as you pour.

Add the olive oil and crushed chillies, and season with pepper, then whisk until combined. Cook for 5 minutes, or according to the pack instructions, then pour into the prepared tart tins. Cool then chill in the fridge for 1 hour, or until firm.

Meanwhile, wrap the beetroots in foil, and bake for 1 hour. Unwrap and leave to cool. Put the beetroots in a blender or food processor and add the garlic, lemon juice, cumin and cream cheese. Blend together until smooth. Season with salt and pepper, then leave to one side.

Bake the polenta tart cases for 30 minutes, or until cooked and crisp. Meanwhile, heat the safflower oil in a large frying pan over a medium-high heat and add the mushrooms. Fry for 10 minutes, or until golden. Season lightly with salt and pepper and remove from the heat. Carefully remove the cooked polenta from the tart tins and put a spoonful of the beetroot spread on top. Put the mushrooms on the spread and serve with the green salad.

Lime & Coconut Cupcakes
(page 112)

Snacks & Treats

Pop some healthy treats into your handbag or lunchbox
to stave away the 3pm craving monster, which can lead
the cleanest of diets into a tailspin of sugar and unhealthy
fats. Whether for mid-morning or mid-afternoon, these
snacks and treats are sure to appeal to the fussy little ones
in your family (or even the bigger ones), and they also
make great party treats. Savouries include Tamari Spiced
Nuts & Seeds (great to sprinkle over salads as well),
Roasted Garlic & Hazelnut Hummus, plus Baked Chilli
Vegetable Crisps or Savoury Biscuits to go with a drink.
Keep your energy up with a bit of fruity sweetness from
Cherry Coconut Crunch Bars or Spiced Apple Tea Cake,
and cool the kids down during a hot afternoon with my
Peach, Orange Blossom & Coconut Ice Pops.

Nutritious nuts and seeds, coated in a lightly spiced, salty sauce, make a perfect party nibble or snack to eat on the run. I keep a small jar of them in my handbag in case of a hunger emergency. They can also be sprinkled over salads.

tamari spiced nuts & *seeds*

Serves: 4
Preparation: 10 minutes
Cooking: 20 minutes,
  plus cooling

150g/5½oz/1 cup almonds
50g/1¾oz/½ cup walnuts
40g/1½oz/¼ cup soya nuts
  or dried edamame
30g/1oz/¼ cup pecan nuts
120g/4¼oz/½ cup pumpkin
  seeds
135g/4¾oz/1 cup sunflower
  seeds
40g/1½oz/¼ cup sesame
  seeds
4 tbsp tamari soy sauce or
  soy sauce, or to taste
1 tsp toasted sesame oil
½ tsp brown sugar or
  coconut sugar
½ tsp ground cinnamon
½ tsp ground allspice

Preheat the oven to 180°C/350°F/Gas 4 and line a baking tray with baking parchment. Put all the nuts and seeds in a large bowl and toss to mix well.

Put the tamari in a small jug and add the sesame oil, sugar and spices, then whisk together. Pour this mixture over the nuts and stir to combine until the nuts are thoroughly coated.

Arrange the nuts evenly over the prepared baking tray and bake for 10 minutes, then shake the baking tray to toss the nuts and return it to the oven to cook for a further 10 minutes. Leave to cool, then serve. Store in an airtight container for up to 4 weeks.

Gluten-free

I love making a huge bowl of these healthy crisps, which can be prepared with other vegetables as well. I often make them using carrot, daikon radish or pumpkin. It's a great way to use up any root or starchy vegetables you have in your vegetable rack.

baked chilli vegetable crisps

Serves: 2
Preparation: 20 minutes
Cooking: 35 minutes

2 beetroots
1 sweet potato
1 parsnip
1 potato
2 tbsp olive oil or melted
  coconut oil
½ tsp sea salt
½ tsp garlic powder
½ tsp dried basil
½ tsp dried oregano
½ tsp dried rosemary
2 tsp crushed chillies
1 tsp paprika

Preheat the oven to 180°C/350°F/Gas 4. Use a wire rack over a baking tray to cook the crisps – this will ensure they are evenly cooked and crisp up well.

Slice all the vegetables into uniformly thin slices, preferably using a mandolin. Put the vegetables in a large bowl and drizzle with the oil. Sprinkle over the flavourings and mix well to cover the slices completely. Arrange the slices on the rack in a single layer and bake for 10–12 minutes until crisp and lightly golden. You may have to do this in batches. Cool and serve. Store in an airtight container for up to 3 days.

Gluten-free   Soya-free   Nut-free   Seed-free   Sugar-free

The Spanish make a picada sauce using hazelnuts, tomato, garlic, bread and oil, and this was the inspiration for my nutty hummus.

roasted garlic & hazelnut hummus

Serves: 2
Preparation: 15 minutes
Cooking: 30 minutes,
** plus cooling**

3 garlic cloves, unpeeled
70g/2½oz/½ cup hazelnuts
400g/14oz/scant 2 cups
  tinned chickpeas, rinsed
  and drained
3 tbsp good-quality extra
  virgin olive oil, plus extra
  to serve
2 tbsp vegetable stock
juice of 1 large lemon
1 tsp sea salt
¼ tsp sweet paprika
pitta bread and vegetable
  sticks, to serve

Preheat the oven to 200°C/400°F/Gas 6 and line a baking tray with baking parchment. Put the garlic on the prepared baking tray and roast for 15 minutes. Add the hazelnuts to the tray and roast for a further 15 minutes.

Leave the hazelnuts and garlic to one side until cool to the touch. Using a clean tea towel, take a handful of hazelnuts and rub off the skins. Repeat with the remaining hazelnuts. Put the nuts in a food processor and squeeze in the roasted garlic from its skin. Process for 2 minutes, or until the hazelnuts have released their oil.

Add the chickpeas and process for 30 seconds, then slowly drizzle in the oil with the blades still turning. Add the stock, lemon juice, salt and paprika, and blend until smooth. Serve drizzled with extra olive oil, with pitta bread and vegetable sticks.

Gluten-free   *Soya-free*   *Seed-free*   *Sugar-free*

roasted afghani *chickpeas*

Serves: 4
Preparation: 5 minutes
Cooking: 40 minutes

1 tbsp olive oil or melted
   coconut oil
zest and juice of 1 lemon
1 tsp paprika
½ tsp turmeric
400g/14oz/scant 2 cups
   tinned chickpeas, rinsed
   and drained
sea salt

Preheat the oven to 180°C/350°F/Gas 4. Line a baking tray with baking parchment. Put the oil in a medium bowl and add the lemon zest and juice, paprika, turmeric and ¼ teaspoon salt, then whisk together well.

Add the chickpeas to the bowl and mix well so that they are covered with the spicy oil. Spread the chickpeas over the prepared baking tray and cook for 40 minutes, shaking the baking tray occasionally to toss the chickpeas, then returning it to the oven to continue cooking. Serve hot with an extra sprinkling of salt.

Gluten-free   *Soya-free*   *Nut-free*   *Seed-free*   *Sugar-free*

coriander *guacamole*

Serves: 4
Preparation: 15 minutes

3 ripe avocados, cut in half,
   pitted and peeled
juice of ½ lemon
juice of ½ lime
4 tbsp finely chopped
   coriander leaves
¼ onion, finely chopped
1 plum or ripe tomato,
   chopped
½ tsp sea salt
¼ tsp chilli powder
warm sourdough bread or
   corn chips, to serve

Put all the ingredients in a large bowl and mash together using a fork until the mixture is your preferred consistency – either smooth or with a few lumps for texture. Serve with sourdough bread or corn chips.

Gluten-free   *Soya-free*   *Nut-free*   *Seed-free*   *Sugar-free*   *Raw*

Soya-free

Seed-free

Sugar-free

potato & coconut samosas

Makes: 16 samosas
Preparation: 20 minutes,
  plus cooling and making
  the relish
Cooking: 30 minutes

100g/3½oz/⅔ cup cashew
  nuts
1 tbsp olive oil or coconut oil
½ onion, finely sliced
2cm/¾in piece fresh root
  ginger, peeled and grated
3 medium potatoes, finely
  chopped
½ tsp ground cumin
½ tsp ground coriander
30g/1oz/¼ cup desiccated
  coconut
3 tbsp coconut cream
4 tbsp chopped coriander
  leaves
8 sheets of vegan filo pastry,
  defrosted if frozen
olive oil, for brushing
sea salt and freshly ground
  black pepper
Tomato Relish (page 48),
  hummus or dairy-free
  yogurt with mint to serve

Preheat the oven to 180°C/350°F/Gas 4 and line a baking sheet with baking parchment. Put the cashew nuts into a blender or food processor and grind into a powder. Leave to one side.

Heat the oil in a large non-stick frying pan over a medium heat, add the onion, ginger and potatoes, and cook for 10 minutes, stirring constantly, or until tender.

Stir in the cumin, ground coriander, cashew nuts, desiccated coconut, coconut cream and coriander leaves, then cook for a further 5 minutes. Season with salt and pepper, then leave to one side to cool.

Lay the filo pastry sheets on a clean surface, and brush lightly with the oil. Lay one filo sheet on top of another and repeat with the remaining sheets to make 4 piles of double-layered filo. Cut each pile into four. Put 4 tablespoonfuls of the mixture into the centre of each square, then brush the edges of the pastry with water.

Fold each square into a triangle, then use your fingers to press the edges together. Transfer to the prepared baking sheet. Brush lightly with oil, and bake for 15 minutes, or until golden. Serve with your chosen accompaniment.

Nut-free

savoury *biscuits*

Makes: 25 biscuits
Preparation: 15 minutes,
  plus 30 minutes chilling
Cooking: 20 minutes,
  plus cooling

125g/4½oz/1 cup plain flour,
  plus extra for dusting
¾ tsp baking powder
¼ tsp sea salt
a large pinch of cayenne
  pepper
¼ tsp brown sugar or
  coconut sugar
1 tbsp nutritional yeast flakes
2 tbsp vegan cream cheese
4 tbsp olive oil
2 tbsp soya milk
½ tsp wholegrain mustard
2 tsp caraway seeds
1 tbsp pumpkin seeds
1 tbsp sesame seeds
freshly ground black pepper
vegan cheeses and pickles,
  to serve

Sift the flour, baking powder, salt and cayenne pepper into a large bowl, then add the sugar and yeast flakes. Lightly season with black pepper. Stir well to combine.

Put the cream cheese in a small bowl and stir in the oil and milk until the mixture becomes creamy and smooth. Pour into the flour mixture and stir to make a dough, adding up to 1½ tablespoons water, if necessary, to bind. Gather the dough together and put it into a small bowl.

Cover and chill in the fridge for 30 minutes. Preheat the oven to 180°C/350°F/Gas 4 and line a baking sheet with baking parchment.

Flour a work surface and roll out the dough to 5mm/¼in thick, then use a 4.5cm/1¾in biscuit cutter to cut out rounds. Put the mustard in a small bowl and add ½ teaspoon water. Mix together, then brush over 5 of the rounds. Sprinkle a pinch of caraway seeds over another 5 rounds and do the same with the pumpkin and sesame seeds, then grind some pepper over the remaining rounds. Gently press the seeds and pepper into the dough, then bake for 15–20 minutes until lightly golden. Carefully transfer the biscuits to a wire rack to cool completely before serving. Serve with cheese and pickles. Store in an airtight container for up to 3 days.

Nut-free

chewy chocolate cookies

Makes: 14 cookies
Preparation: 15 minutes,
 plus 10 minutes soaking
Cooking: 15 minutes,
 plus cooling

1 vanilla pod
1 tbsp chia seeds
250ml/9fl oz/1 cup safflower
 oil, or sunflower oil or
 melted coconut oil
180g/6¼oz/1 cup brown
 sugar or coconut sugar
310g/11oz/2½ cups plain
 flour
1 tsp baking powder
60g/2¼oz/½ cup cocoa
 powder or raw cacao
 powder
150g/5½oz vegan dark
 chocolate, chopped into
 small chunks

Preheat the oven to 180°C/350°F/Gas 4 and line a baking sheet with baking parchment. Split the vanilla pod in half lengthways and scrape out the seeds. Reserve the pod for another use. Leave the seeds to one side. Put the chia seeds in a small bowl and add 2 tablespoons water. Leave to soak for 10 minutes to form a gel.

Put the oil in a heatproof bowl over a pan of gently simmering water. Add the sugar and whisk together until the sugar has dissolved. Add the vanilla seeds and chia-seed gel. Mix well and leave to one side.

In a large bowl, sift together the flour, baking powder and cocoa powder. Add the chocolate chunks and stir to combine. Make a small well in the centre and add the oil mixture. Stir well. The dough should be soft and not too dry, but firm enough to hold its shape. Add a little water if necessary.

Scoop out a large heaped teaspoonful of the dough and put it on to the prepared baking sheet. Use a fork to flatten the dough slightly. Repeat with the remaining dough, spaced evenly apart. Bake for 12–15 minutes until golden. Leave to cool on the baking sheet for 5 minutes, then transfer to a wire rack to cool completely before serving.

raw sesame *fudge slice*

Makes: 16 squares
Preparation: 5 minutes,
  plus 3 hours chilling

150g/5½oz/1 cup sesame
  seeds
60g/2¼oz/½ cup raw cacao
  powder
2 tbsp carob powder
100ml/3½fl oz/generous
  ⅓ cup agave syrup or
  brown rice syrup
4 tbsp coconut oil, melted

Put the sesame seeds into a blender or food processor and
process until ground. Add the remaining ingredients and blend
until well combined. Press into a 30 × 23cm/12 × 9in baking tray
and chill in the fridge for 2–3 hours until firm. Cut into squares
and serve.

Gluten-free   *Soya-free*   *Nut-free*   *Raw*

quinoa *choc - crackle slice*

Makes: 16 squares
Preparation: 10 minutes,
  plus 2 hours chilling

375ml/13fl oz/1½ cups
  coconut nectar, or
  90g/3¼oz/½ cup brown
  sugar or coconut sugar
250g/9oz/4 cups puffed
  quinoa
2 tbsp coconut oil, melted
½ tsp sea salt
60g/2¼oz/¼ cup almond
  butter
2 tbsp raw cacao powder or
  cocoa powder

If using sugar, put it in a small bowl and add 125ml/4fl oz/½ cup
warm water. Stir to dissolve. Tip the puffed quinoa into a shallow
non-stick 23 × 23cm/9 × 9in traybake tin and leave to one side.
Put the coconut nectar or sugar water in a bowl and add the oil,
salt, almond butter and cacao powder. Stir well to combine.

Pour over the puffed quinoa and stir well. Press the mixture down
firmly and chill for 2 hours. Slice into squares using a sharp knife,
then serve. Store in an airtight container for up to 2 weeks.

Gluten-free   *Soya-free*   *Seed-free*

Rich in triglycerides (medium-chain fatty acids) from the coconut, these bars are perfect for an energy boost. They are also high in vitamin C and healthful flavonoids, and are so tasty that kids (both small and big) will devour them without knowing how healthy they are.

cherry coconut *crunch bars*

Makes: 12 bars
Preparation: 15 minutes,
** plus 30 minutes chilling**

380g/13½oz/2½ cups
  almonds
50g/1¾oz/⅓ cup chia seeds
120g/4¼oz/½ cup cherries,
  pitted
40g/1½oz/¼ cup dried
  cherries, dried cranberries
  or raisins
100g/3½oz/½ cup dried
  medjool dates, pitted
40g/1½ oz/¼ cup cacao
  nibs or chopped dark vegan
  chocolate
30g/1oz/¼ cup desiccated
  coconut
1 tbsp brown sugar or
  coconut sugar
1 tbsp melted coconut oil

Line a 23 × 23cm/9 × 9in baking tray with baking parchment. Put the almonds into a food processor and add the chia seeds, fresh and dried cherries, dates, cacao nibs and desiccated coconut. Pulse until the almonds are crushed, then blend on high speed for 10 seconds.

Put the sugar in a bowl and add the oil plus 70ml/2¼fl oz/ scant ⅓ cup warm water. Whisk together until the sugar dissolves. Add to the food processor and blend for a further 10 seconds, or until combined.

Press the mixture into the prepared tray to a thickness of 2.5cm/1in, then chill in the fridge for 30 minutes or until firm. Cut the mixture into 12 bars and serve. Store in an airtight container in the fridge for up to 1 week.

Gluten-free   *Soya-free*   *Raw*

Two of my favourite foods are brought together in these muffins. Chai spices and banana are perfect partners, and are superb when baked in a warm and delicious muffin. Lighter than cake, but denser than cupcakes, these muffins are the best of both worlds.

chai-spiced banana *muffins*

Makes: 12 muffins
Preparation: 15 minutes
Cooking: 25 minutes,
  plus cooling

125ml/4fl oz/½ cup
  coconut milk
1 tsp cider vinegar
80ml/2½fl oz/⅓ cup
  safflower oil, sunflower oil
  or melted coconut oil
2 ripe bananas, mashed
1 tsp vanilla extract
½ tsp ground cardamom
½ tsp ground cloves
1 tsp ground cinnamon
1 tsp ground ginger
½ tsp ground allspice
½ tsp black pepper
250g/9oz/2 cups plain flour
½ tsp baking powder
75g/2½oz/¾ cup pecan
  nuts, roughly chopped,
  plus extra for decoration

Preheat the oven to 190°C/375°F/Gas 5, and line a 12-cup muffin tray with paper muffin cases. Pour the coconut milk into a small jug and add the cider vinegar, then whisk together. Leave to one side.

Put the oil in a large bowl and add the bananas, vanilla extract and spices. Stir well. Sift in half the flour and the baking powder and stir in gently, then sift in the remaining flour and briefly stir again. Fold in the pecan nuts.

Divide the mixture evenly into the paper cases and scatter a few chopped pecan nuts over the top. Bake for 20–25 minutes until firm on top and a skewer inserted into the centre comes out clean. Leave to cool in the tin on a wire rack for 5 minutes, then turn out on to the wire rack to cool completely before serving. Store in an airtight container for up to 4 days.

Soya-free   Sugar-free

These brownies can be made quickly and easily by just whizzing them up in your blender.

chocolate goji *brownies*

Makes: 12 squares
Preparation: 5 minutes,
  plus 5 minutes soaking
Cooking: 45 minutes,
  plus cooling

50g/1¾oz/½ cup goji berries, dried dates or apricots, chopped, plus extra to decorate (optional)
1 vanilla pod
120g/4¼oz/1 cup gluten-free flour blend
1 tsp sea salt
90g/3¼oz/¾ cup cocoa powder or raw cacao powder
90g/3¼oz/½ cup brown sugar or coconut sugar
185ml/6fl oz/¾ cup safflower oil, sunflower oil or melted coconut oil
4 tbsp ground flaxseed

Preheat the oven to 180°C/350°F/Gas 4. Put the goji berries in a small bowl and cover with water. Leave to soak for 5 minutes, then drain in a colander. Split the vanilla pod in half lengthways and scrape out the seeds. Reserve the pod for another use.

Sift the flour, salt and cocoa powder into a food processor and add the sugar and vanilla seeds. Process on high speed for 20 seconds. (Alternatively, put the ingredients in a mixing bowl and stir thoroughly.) Add the oil, ground flaxseed, goji berries and 2 tablespoons water, then process for 20 seconds, or stir well, until combined.

Pour the mixture into a 23 × 23cm/9 × 9in non-stick traybake tin. Scatter with extra fruit, if using, and cook for 40–45 minutes until a skewer inserted into the centre comes out clean. Leave to cool, then cut into 12 squares before serving. Store in an airtight container for up to 1 week.

Gluten-free   *Soya-free*   *Nut-free*

lime & coconut *cupcakes*

Makes: 14 cupcakes
Preparation: 30 minutes, plus
   making the optional milk
Cooking: 20 minutes, plus
   cooling

210g/7½oz/1¾ cups plain
   flour
2 tsp baking powder
a pinch of sea salt
140g/5oz/¾ cup brown
   sugar or coconut sugar
30g/1oz/⅓ cup desiccated
   coconut, plus extra to
   decorate
250ml/9fl oz/1 cup coconut
   milk or Almond Milk
   (page 20)
125ml/4fl oz/½ cup safflower
   oil or sunflower oil
1 tsp almond extract
1 tsp vanilla paste
1 tbsp cider vinegar

ICING
90g/3¼oz/⅓ cup vegan
   margarine
4 tsp Almond Milk
finely grated zest of 1 lime,
   plus extra to decorate
½ tsp lime juice
250g/9oz/2 cups icing sugar

Preheat the oven to 180°C/350°F/Gas 4 and line 14 muffin cups with paper cases. Sift the flour, baking powder and salt into a large bowl and stir in the sugar and coconut. Pour the milk into a separate bowl and add the oil, almond extract, vanilla paste and vinegar. Mix well, then pour the milk mixture into the dry ingredients and stir with a wooden spoon until just combined.

Divide the mixture into the paper cases until three-quarters full. Bake for 18 minutes, or until well risen and a skewer inserted into the centre of a cupcake comes out clean. Remove the cupcakes from the tin and transfer them to a wire rack to cool completely.

To make the icing, put the margarine, milk, lime zest and juice in a large mixing bowl and sift in the icing sugar. Beat, using a whisk or hand-held electric mixer, until light and fluffy. Swirl the icing on to the top of each cupcake. Top with a sprinkling of coconut and lime zest, and serve.

Soya-free

spiced apple *tea cake*

Serves: 8–10
Preparation: 15 minutes, plus
10 minutes soaking and
making the milk
Cooking: 1¼ hours, plus
cooling

2 tbsp chia seeds
150ml/5fl oz/scant ⅔ cup
  safflower oil, sunflower oil
  or melted coconut oil, plus
  extra for greasing
185g/6½oz/1½ cups plain
  flour
2 tsp baking powder
1½ tbsp ground ginger
1 tsp ground cinnamon
185g/6½oz/1 cup brown
  sugar or coconut sugar
60ml/2fl oz/¼ cup Almond
  Milk (page 20)

APPLE TOPPING
185g/6½oz/1 cup brown
  sugar or coconut sugar
grated zest and juice of
  1 lemon
1 tsp ground cinnamon
2 eating apples, peeled,
  cored and thinly sliced

Put the chia seeds in a small bowl and add 4 tablespoons water. Leave to soak for 10 minutes to form a gel. Preheat the oven to 180°C/350°F/Gas 4 and lightly grease a 23cm/9in cake tin.

To make the apple topping, pour 750ml/26fl oz/3 cups water into a small saucepan over a medium heat and add the sugar, lemon zest and juice, and the cinnamon. Stir gently, then bring to a gentle boil, and add the apple slices. Cook for 10 minutes, or until the apples are tender but still holding their shape, then remove from the liquid using a slotted spoon. Leave the apples to one side to cool, discarding the cooking liquid.

Meanwhile, sift the flour, baking powder, ginger and cinnamon into a large mixing bowl and stir in the sugar. Pour the oil into the bowl with the chia-seed gel and add 4 tablespoons water and the milk. Mix together well, then pour this mixture into the dry ingredients in the mixing bowl. Stir until just incorporated, but do not over-mix.

Tip the batter into the prepared tin and level the top. Lay the apple slices on the top, starting at the outside edge and working into the centre. Bake for 55 minutes, or until the cake springs back when pressed. Leave to cool in the tin on a wire rack, then remove from the tin and serve.

This beautiful, richly flavoured loaf takes very little time to prepare using your blender.

almond & coconut loaf

Makes: 1 loaf (10 slices)
Preparation: 10 minutes,
  plus 10 minutes soaking,
  and making the milk and
  optional spread
Cooking: 1 hour, plus cooling

1 tbsp chia seeds
250ml/9fl oz/1 cup safflower
  oil, or sunflower oil or
  melted coconut oil, plus
  extra for greasing
grated zest of 1 orange
140g/5oz/¾ cup brown
  sugar or coconut sugar
375g/13oz/3 cups plain flour
2 tsp baking powder
90g/3¼oz/1 cup desiccated
  coconut
70g/2½oz/⅔ cup ground
  almonds
250ml/9fl oz/1 cup Almond
  Milk (page 20)
berries or Fruit & Pumpkin
  Spread (page 26), to serve

Put the chia seeds in a small bowl and add 3 tablespoons water. Leave to soak for 10 minutes to form a gel. Preheat the oven to 180°C/350°F/Gas 4, and grease a 23 × 10cm/9 × 4in loaf tin.

Put the oil in a blender or food processor and add the orange zest and sugar. Add the chia-seed gel and blend until mixed. Sift in the flour and baking powder and add the coconut, ground almonds and milk, then blend on high speed for 30 seconds, or until combined.

Pour into the prepared loaf tin and bake for 1 hour, or until the loaf springs back when pressed. Leave the loaf to cool in the tin, then turn it on to a wire rack. Serve with fresh berries or a large spoonful of spread. Store in an airtight container for up to 1 week.

Soya-free

Gluten-free *Soya-free* *Seed-free* *Sugar-free*

peach, orange blossom &
coconut ice pops

Makes: 6 ice pops
Preparation: 5 minutes,
  plus 20 minutes soaking
  and 4 hours freezing, and
  making the milk

2 fresh or dried medjool
  dates, pitted
4 large peaches, cut in half,
  pitted and chopped
200ml/7fl oz/scant 1 cup
  coconut milk
200ml/7fl oz/scant 1 cup
  Almond Milk (page 20)
1 tsp orange blossom water

If using dried dates, put them in a small bowl and cover with water. Leave to soak for 20 minutes, then drain in a colander.

Put all the ingredients into a blender or food processor and blend until smooth. Pour the mixture into 6 lolly moulds and freeze for 3–4 hours until firm. Serve.

Main Meals

The main meal of the day is a chance for couples or families to sit together and chat over their favourite dishes – steamy bowls of robust soups, home-made burgers and spicy curries. There's nothing better than to fill up on a wholesome dish that doesn't feel heavy on the stomach, and these plant-based recipes certainly fit the bill. Quinoa Stuffed Peppers are spicy and have a sweet and nutty edge, Moussaka with Cottage-Feta Cheese is based on vegetables rather than pasta, and South African Sweet Potato Stew is spicy and warming. You'll find noodle and risotto dishes as well as an appealing Rustic Tart with Spinach Pesto – and you can save any leftovers for lunch tomorrow.

Thai Green Aubergine Curry
(page 134).

This is a fast and easy main-course soup that looks and tastes inviting. Make it smooth or leave it crunchy.

chilli peanut & coconut soup

Serves: 4
Preparation: 15 minutes
Cooking: 35 minutes

200g/7oz tempeh, cut into
  cubes
2 tbsp tamari soy sauce or
  soy sauce
2 tsp crushed chillies
2 tbsp toasted sesame oil
1 onion, finely chopped
1 red pepper, deseeded and
  chopped
3 garlic cloves, crushed
1 small red chilli, deseeded
  and finely chopped
160g/5¾oz/1 cup unsalted
  roasted peanuts, roughly
  chopped, plus 2 tbsp
  chopped peanuts to serve
400ml/14fl oz/1½ cups
  coconut milk
4 spring onions, thinly sliced
100g/3½oz/generous 1 cup
  bean sprouts
50g/1¾oz mangetout
  or green beans, sliced
  diagonally
1 handful of coriander leaves
cooked brown rice or naan
  bread, to serve

Put the tempeh in a large bowl and add 1 tablespoon of the tamari and the crushed chillies. Toss well. Heat 1 tablespoon of the oil in a heavy-based saucepan over a medium heat and cook the tempeh for 5 minutes, or until golden brown, turning regularly. Remove and leave to one side. Heat the remaining oil in the pan and add the onion, pepper and garlic. Cook for 5–8 minutes until softened. Add the chilli and roasted peanuts, and stir constantly for 2 minutes, until fragrant.

Add the remaining tamari, 600ml/21fl oz/scant 2½ cups water and the coconut milk, and bring the soup gently to the boil. Lower the heat, and simmer for 15 minutes, or until the soup thickens slightly.

If you prefer a smooth soup, use a hand blender to process it to your preferred consistency. Divide into bowls, and add the tempeh, spring onions, bean sprouts, mangetout and coriander, then sprinkle some chopped peanuts over the top. Serve with brown rice.

Gluten-free   *Sugar-free*

I have made a number of tweaks to this recipe over the years to give it a more complex flavour. Coconut cream is a staple ingredient in Asian dishes and is a wonderful way to add richness and depth.

coconut & red lentil dhal

Serves: 4
Preparation: 15 minutes,
plus making the parathas
Cooking: 45 minutes

1 tbsp olive oil or coconut oil
1 large onion, chopped
3 garlic cloves, crushed
1cm/½in piece fresh root
  ginger, peeled and grated
2 tsp cumin seeds
1 tsp yellow mustard seeds
2 tsp garam masala
1 tsp ground turmeric
2 tsp dried fenugreek leaves
1 tsp ground cumin
1 tsp ground coriander
1 tsp crushed chillies
  (optional)
250g/9oz/1 cup red lentils,
  rinsed and drained
400ml/14fl oz/1½ cups
  coconut cream
400g/14oz/scant 1⅔ cups
  tinned chopped tomatoes
1 tsp sea salt
juice of 1 lime
fresh coriander and Garlic
  Parathas (page 27) or
  cooked brown rice, to serve

Heat the oil in a large saucepan over a medium-high heat and add the onion and garlic. Cook for 5–8 minutes, stirring frequently, until softened. Add the ginger, cumin seeds and mustard seeds, and cook for a further 2 minutes, or until the seeds begin to pop. Add 1 tablespoon water, if the mixture is catching on the pan, and then add the garam masala, turmeric, fenugreek, ground cumin, coriander and crushed chillies, if using. Stir until the mixture forms a thick, brown paste.

Add the lentils, coconut cream, tomatoes and 250ml/9fl oz/ 1 cup water. Bring to the boil, then reduce the heat to a simmer and cook for 20 minutes, stirring frequently. Add the salt and lime juice, and cook for a further 10 minutes. Serve with a sprig of coriander and parathas.

Gluten-free   *Soya-free*   *Seed-free*   *Sugar-free*

pan-fried sage & *basil gnocchi*

Serves: 4
Preparation: 15 minutes,
  plus 10 minutes resting
  and making the cheese
Cooking: 45 minutes

500g/1lb 2oz floury potatoes,
  such as Desiree or King
  Edward, cut into dice
180g/6¼oz/1½ cups plain
  flour, plus extra if needed
  and for dusting
1 tbsp finely chopped sage
  leaves
1 tbsp finely chopped
  basil leaves
1 tbsp safflower oil or
  sunflower oil
150g/5½oz/1 cup pitted
  mixed green and black
  olives, chopped
1 red chilli, deseeded and
  thinly sliced lengthways
100g/3½oz baby spinach
  leaves
80g/2¾oz/½ cup drained
  sun-dried tomatoes in oil,
  chopped
200g/7oz/1 cup bottled or
  tinned artichoke hearts
1 handful of basil leaves, torn
200g/7oz Herbed Almond
  Cheese (page 22), crumbled
sea salt and freshly ground
  black pepper

Put the potatoes in a steamer set over a pan of boiling water and steam over a medium heat for 15–20 minutes until soft. Preheat the oven to 100°C/200°F/Gas ½ and put a baking tray inside to warm.

Put the potatoes in a bowl, mash them and sift in 150g/5½oz/1¼ cups flour, the herbs and add a good pinch of salt. Mix by hand until just combined, adding the remaining flour. Turn the dough on to a floured surface and knead for 1 minute. If the dough is sticky, add more flour, 1 teaspoon at a time, until the dough is soft and workable. Leave to rest for 10 minutes.

Bring a large saucepan of salted water to the boil over a high heat, then reduce to medium-high. Divide the dough into four pieces and roll them into long sausage shapes. Slice each piece into 2cm/¾in pieces to make gnocchi. Lower the gnocchi in batches into the boiling water using a slotted spoon, and cook for 5 minutes, or until they float to the surface. Remove from the pan as they cook and lay them on the baking tray and keep them warm while you cook the remaining gnocchi.

Heat the oil in a large, non-stick frying pan over a medium-high heat and fry the gnocchi in batches, keeping the cooked gnocchi warm on the tray. Add the olives and chilli to the pan, and cook for 5 minutes. Add the spinach, tomatoes, artichokes and basil. Return the gnocchi to the pan and gently toss with the vegetables. Season with pepper and serve with the cheese.

Gluten-free   Soya-free   Seed-free   Sugar-free

quinoa stuffed peppers

Serves: 4
Preparation: 15 minutes, plus
   10 minutes soaking and
   making the sauce
Cooking: 1 hour 5 minutes

2 fresh or dried medjool
  dates, pitted and chopped
4 red peppers
1 tbsp olive oil or coconut oil
1 onion, chopped
1 garlic clove, crushed
1 tsp ground turmeric
¼ tsp ground cinnamon
1 tsp cumin seeds
½ tsp ground cardamom
100g/3½oz/½ cup red
  quinoa, rinsed and drained
100g/3½oz/½ cup white
  quinoa, rinsed and drained
400g/14oz/scant 2 cups
  tinned chickpeas, rinsed
  and drained
1 dried fig, finely chopped
4 ready-to-eat dried apricots,
  finely chopped
1 large handful of coriander
  leaves, chopped
3 tbsp pine nuts
sea salt
Chermoula Sauce (page 85),
  to serve

Preheat the oven to 180°C/350°F/Gas 4 and line a baking tray or ovenproof dish with baking parchment. If using dried dates, put the chopped dates in a small bowl and cover with water. Leave to soak for 10 minutes, then drain in a sieve.

Cut the peppers in half through the stalk and remove the seeds and pith from inside. Leave the peppers to one side.

Heat the oil in a non-stick frying pan over a medium heat. Fry the onion and garlic for 7–8 minutes until beginning to soften, then add the turmeric, cinnamon, cumin seeds and cardamom. Leave to one side.

Meanwhile, pour 500ml/17fl oz/2 cups boiling water into a medium saucepan over a high heat and add both types of quinoa. Boil for 15 minutes, or until tender and translucent. Drain the quinoa in a sieve and rinse, then drain thoroughly and tip into a large bowl. Stir in the onion mixture, the chickpeas, fig, dates, apricots, coriander and pine nuts. Season with salt.

Spoon into the peppers and bake for 30–40 minutes until tender. Serve with chermoula sauce.

While in Thailand, I learned that the essence of Thai food is in the balance of sweetness, saltiness, spiciness and sourness – I have aimed for that perfect relationship here.

khao soi – thai curry noodles

Serves: 4
**Preparation: 15 minutes, plus
  making the curry paste**
Cooking: 20 minutes

1 tbsp toasted sesame oil
150g/5½oz/1 cup cashew
  nuts
2 tbsp Thai Red Curry Paste
  (page 25)
2 courgettes, cut in half and
  sliced
1 carrot, chopped
400g/14oz button
  mushrooms, sliced
2½ tbsp tomato purée
400ml/14fl oz/1½ cups
  tinned coconut milk
2 tsp curry powder
3 tbsp tamari soy sauce or
  soy sauce
2 tsp brown sugar or coconut
  sugar
150g/5½oz rice noodles
100g/3½oz/1 cup bean
  sprouts, plus extra to serve
4 tbsp coriander leaves
4 spring onions, diagonally
  sliced
lime wedges, to serve

Heat the sesame oil in a large saucepan over a medium-high heat. Add the cashew nuts and cook for 3–4 minutes, stirring regularly, until golden brown. Remove the nuts from the pan and drain on kitchen paper. Leave to one side. Reduce the heat to medium.

Add the Thai curry paste to the pan and stir constantly for 30 seconds, or until fragrant. Add the courgettes, carrot, mushrooms and tomato purée, and stir well. Pour in the coconut milk and 500ml/17fl oz/2 cups water, the curry powder, tamari and sugar, and bring gently to the boil. Reduce the heat and simmer for 10 minutes, or until the carrot is tender.

Meanwhile, put the rice noodles in a heatproof bowl and pour boiling water over to cover generously. Gently move the noodles in the water, using a fork, and leave for 5–6 minutes until soft.

Add the bean sprouts to the vegetable mixture just before serving, stir well and remove from the heat. Drain the noodles in a colander and divide into four large serving bowls. Ladle the soup and vegetables over the noodles, and top with the fried cashew nuts, coriander, spring onions and extra bean sprouts. Serve with the wedges of lime.

Gluten-free

Gluten-free Soya-free Seed-free Sugar-free

moussaka with cottage-feta cheese

Serves: 4
Preparation: 30 minutes,
  plus making the cheese
Cooking: 1 hour 15 minutes

4 tbsp olive oil or coconut oil,
  plus extra for greasing
1 large aubergine, thinly
  sliced
2 courgettes, thinly sliced
  lengthways
2 potatoes, thinly sliced
1 onion, chopped
2 garlic cloves, crushed
900g/2lb/4 cups tinned
  chopped tomatoes
200g/7oz/1 cup White
  Cottage-Feta Cheese (page
  21), crumbled
200g/7oz/1 cup tinned
  brown lentils, rinsed and
  drained
500ml/17fl oz/2 cups passata
sea salt and freshly ground
  black pepper
green salad and olives,
  to serve

Preheat the oven to 200°C/400°F/Gas 6, and lightly grease a 23 × 33cm/9 × 13in ovenproof dish. Heat 1 tablespoon of the oil in a non-stick frying pan over a medium heat. Working in batches, lightly brown the aubergine, courgettes and potatoes on both sides, adding more oil as necessary. As each batch finishes, transfer to a colander lined with kitchen paper and leave to drain.

Meanwhile, heat the remaining oil in a saucepan and cook the onion and garlic for for 5–8 minutes until softened, then stir in the tomatoes and bring to the boil. Season with salt and pepper, and cook for 5 minutes.

Add a layer of aubergine, courgettes and potatoes over the base of the prepared dish and top with 4 tablespoonfuls of the tomato mixture, then scatter over 4 tablespoonfuls of cheese and 4 tablespoonfuls of lentils. Season lightly. Pour over enough passata for a light covering.

Make 3 more layers in the same way, pressing the layers down firmly. Add all the remaining passata to the top layer. Bake for 35 minutes, or until thoroughly heated through and bubbling at the sides. Serve with a big green salad and plenty of olives.

Gluten-free Soya-free Seed-free

baked polenta with tomato &
basil sauce

Serves: 4
Preparation: 15 minutes
Cooking: 1 hour

1 tbsp plus 1 tsp olive oil or
 coconut oil, plus extra for
 greasing
150g/5½oz/1 cup polenta
30g/1oz/¼ cup ground
 almonds
1l/35fl oz/4 cups vegetable
 stock
2 tbsp lemon juice
60g/2¼oz/heaped ⅓ cup
 pine nuts
1 onion, chopped
1 garlic clove, crushed
400g/14oz/scant 1⅔ cups
 tinned chopped tomatoes
1 handful of basil leaves, plus
 1 tbsp chopped basil leaves
1 tsp dried oregano
½ tsp crushed chillies
½ tsp brown sugar or
 coconut sugar
sea salt and freshly ground
 black pepper

Preheat the oven to 180°C/350°F/Gas 4 and lightly grease a
2l/70fl oz/8 cup shallow ovenproof dish. Put the polenta and
ground almonds in a bowl and add the stock, a pinch of salt
and the lemon juice. Stir well to combine, then pour into the
ovenproof dish and spread out evenly (the ground almonds will
float to the top and the polenta will sink to the bottom). Bake for
45 minutes.

Meanwhile, put the pine nuts in a large saucepan over a medium
heat and dry-toast for 1–2 minutes or until golden, shaking the
pan frequently. Tip on to a small plate and leave to one side.

Add 1 tablespoon of the oil to the pan and add the onion and
garlic, and cook for 5–8 minutes until softened. Add the
tomatoes, 1 tablespoon chopped basil, the oregano, crushed
chillies and sugar, and add enough water to just cover. Season
with salt and pepper, and bring to a gentle boil, then reduce the
heat and simmer for 15 minutes.

Remove the semi-set polenta from the oven and stir in the
1 teaspoon oil. If using coconut oil, this will melt immediately.
Bake for a further 15 minutes, or until crisp on top. The ground
almonds will create a delicious crust. Spoon the tomato sauce
over the polenta and scatter over the toasted pine nuts and the
basil leaves. Add a grinding of black pepper and serve.

Gluten-free Soya-free Seed-free Sugar-free

mushroom & pea coconut korma

Serves: 4
Preparation: 15 minutes,
  plus making the optional
  parathas
Cooking: 1 hour

1 tsp olive oil or coconut oil
1 onion, chopped
3 garlic cloves, crushed
1 tsp cumin seeds
1 tsp yellow mustard seeds
2 tsp garam masala
1 tbsp ground turmeric
1 tbsp dried fenugreek leaves
200g/7oz mixed mushrooms,
  sliced or cut in half, if large
375ml/13fl oz/1½ cups
  coconut milk
400g/14oz/1⅔ cups tinned
  chopped tomatoes
200g/7oz tomatoes, chopped
120g/4¼oz broccoli florets,
  cut in half
150g/5½oz/1 cup shelled
  green peas or frozen peas
150g/5½oz/1 cup almonds,
  roughly chopped
cooked brown rice, quinoa or
  Garlic Parathas (page 27),
  to serve

Heat the oil in a large saucepan over a medium heat and add the onion and garlic. Cook for 5–8 minutes until softened. Add the cumin seeds and mustard seeds, and stir-fry for 30 seconds, or until they begin to pop. Add the garam masala, turmeric and fenugreek, and stir to combine.

Add the mushrooms, coconut milk, 125ml/4fl oz/½ cup water and the tinned and fresh tomatoes, then stir and bring to a gentle boil, stirring frequently. Cook over a medium-low heat for 20 minutes, or until the mushrooms are soft and the sauce has thickened. Add the broccoli and peas, and cook for a further 10 minutes. Stir in the chopped almonds just before serving. Serve with brown rice.

There are three types of aubergine used in this fragrant dish. You should be able to find them in an Asian grocer's or market, but if not, you can substitute them with 450g/1lb regular aubergines, cut into cubes.

thai green aubergine curry

Serves: 4
Preparation: 10 minutes, plus making the curry paste
Cooking: 20 minutes

1 tsp olive oil or coconut oil
3 tbsp Thai Green Curry Paste (page 25)
400ml/14fl oz/1½ cups coconut milk
100g/3½oz aubergine, cut into cubes
250g/9oz baby aubergines
120g/4¼oz pea aubergines, or baby aubergines cut into quarters
1 carrot, thinly sliced
1 courgette, sliced
½ tsp tamari soy sauce or soy sauce, or to taste
1 tsp brown sugar or coconut sugar, or to taste
350g/12oz firm tofu, cut into cubes
2 tbsp fresh lime juice
2 kaffir lime leaves, torn
sea salt
cooked brown rice, to serve

Heat the oil in a large saucepan over a medium heat and add the curry paste. Cook for 1 minute, stirring frequently, until fragrant.

Add the coconut milk, 250ml/9fl oz/1 cup water, all the aubergines, the carrot and courgette, and bring gently to the boil. Reduce the heat, and add the tamari and sugar. Season with salt. Adjust those three seasonings to taste, to balance the salty-spicy-sour-sweet flavours.

Add the tofu and simmer for 10 minutes. Add the lime juice and kaffir lime leaves, then serve over brown rice.

Gluten-free   Seed-free

Traditionally a Hare Krishna dish, this curry is so simple to make, and it tastes good and is inexpensive.

curried cabbage with *potatoes*

Serves: 4
Preparation: 15 minutes,
plus making the dhal
and parathas
Cooking: 25 minutes

2 tbsp plus 2 tsp olive oil or
  coconut oil
120g/4¼oz/¾ cup peanuts
2 tbsp curry powder
3 large potatoes, unpeeled
  and cut into cubes
1 garlic clove, crushed
1cm/½in piece fresh root
  ginger, peeled and grated
1 tsp garam masala
½ tsp ground turmeric
½ tsp brown sugar or
  coconut sugar
450g/1lb green cabbage,
  thinly sliced
250g/9oz/1 cup tinned
  chopped tomatoes
185ml/6fl oz/¾ cup
  vegetable stock
sea salt
Coconut & Red Lentil Dhal
  (page 123) and Garlic
  Parathas (page 27), to serve

Heat 2 teaspoons of the oil in a large frying pan over a medium-high heat and add the peanuts and curry powder. Mix together well and cook for 5 minutes, stirring frequently. Remove the spicy peanuts from the pan and leave to one side.

Heat the remaining oil in the same pan and add the potatoes. Cook for 10 minutes, stirring frequently to ensure they don't catch on the base of the pan, or until lightly golden brown and partly cooked. Remove from the pan and leave to one side.

Add the garlic, ginger, garam masala, turmeric and sugar to the pan. Stir quickly, to release the flavours, then add the cabbage. Stir to coat, then return the potatoes to the pan followed by the tomatoes and stock. Season with salt.

Reduce the heat to low, cover the pan and simmer gently for 10 minutes, or until the cabbage is tender and the potatoes are cooked through. Top with the spicy peanuts and serve with dhal and parathas.

Gluten-free   Soya-free   Seed-free

This hearty dish is flavoured with ginger, and the peanut butter gives it richness.

south african sweet potato stew

Serves: 4
Preparation: 15 minutes
Cooking: 50 minutes

2 tsp olive oil or coconut oil
4 garlic cloves, crushed
1 red pepper, deseeded and
  cut into dice
1 tsp crushed chillies
½ tsp ground cinnamon
1 tsp ground ginger
1 tsp brown sugar or coconut
  sugar
300g/10½oz sweet potato,
  cut into cubes
400g/14oz/scant 1⅔ cups
  tinned chopped tomatoes
250ml/9fl oz/1 cup vegetable
  stock
2 tsp tomato purée
1 tbsp peanut butter
400g/14oz/2 cups tinned red
  kidney beans, rinsed and
  drained
2 tbsp chopped coriander
  leaves
sea salt and freshly ground
  black pepper
cooked brown rice, to serve

Heat the oil in a large, non-stick saucepan over a medium heat and add the garlic and pepper. Cook for 10 minutes, or until tender. Add the spices and stir until fragrant.

Add the sugar, sweet potato, tomatoes, stock, tomato purée and peanut butter, and stir well. Bring gently to the boil, then reduce the heat and simmer for 25 minutes, or until the sweet potato is tender.

Add the kidney beans and cook for a further 10 minutes, adding more water, 1 tablespoon at a time, if the mixture looks a little dry. Season with salt and pepper. Scatter over the coriander and serve with brown rice.

Gluten-free   Soya-free   Seed-free

The whole family will enjoy this hearty meal and everyone can prepare their own burritos. Serve with iced tea.

spicy mexican *burritos*

Serves: 4
Preparation: 15 minutes, plus making the optional cheese and guacamole
Cooking: 40 minutes, plus cooling

200g/7oz/1 cup brown rice
400g/14oz/2 cups tinned red kidney beans, rinsed and drained
2 garlic cloves, crushed
500ml/17fl oz/2 cups passata
2 plum tomatoes, chopped
1 tbsp tomato purée
1 tsp ground cumin
1 tsp ground turmeric
1 tsp chilli powder
juice of 1 lemon
juice of 1 lime
1 large handful of coriander leaves, finely chopped
1 large handful of parsley leaves, finely chopped
8 flour tortillas
100g/3½oz mixed salad leaves, plus extra to serve
100g/3½oz Herbed Almond Cheese (optional) (page 22), plus extra to serve
Coriander Guacamole (page 99), to serve
sea salt

Pour 500ml/17fl oz/2 cups boiling water into a large saucepan, add a pinch of salt and the rice, and return to the boil. Cook for 35–40 minutes, or according to the pack instructions, until tender. Drain in a colander and leave to one side to cool slightly.

Put the kidney beans in a medium saucepan over a medium heat and add the garlic, passata, tomatoes, tomato purée, cumin, turmeric and chilli powder. Mix together well. Bring gently to the boil then remove from the heat. Leave to one side to cool slightly.

Put the cooked brown rice in a bowl and add the lemon and lime juice, coriander and parsley. Mix well.

To make the burritos, put 1 tablespoon rice mixture on to a tortilla, top with 1 tablespoon kidney beans and then add some salad leaves and cheese, if using. Roll up the tortilla, tucking in the bottom edge and leaving the top open. Serve with cheese, if you like, guacamole and salad.

Soya-free *Nut-free* *Seed-free* *Sugar-free*

Nut-free   *Sugar-free*

udon noodle bowl

Serves: 4
Preparation: 15 minutes
Cooking: 25 minutes

350g/12oz udon noodles
3 tbsp toasted sesame oil
400g/14oz firm smoked tofu,
　cut into cubes
2 tbsp sesame seeds
100g/3½oz shallots, sliced
2 tsp rice vinegar
2 tsp mirin or rice wine
　vinegar
2 tbsp miso
8 pak choi, cut in half
　lengthways
100g/3½oz enoki
　mushrooms, trimmed, or
　baby button mushrooms,
　cut in half
sea salt
12 chives, whole or chopped,
　to serve

Bring a large saucepan of salted water to the boil over a high heat. Add the noodles and cook for 8–10 minutes, or according to the pack instructions, until tender. Drain in a colander, rinse with cold water and drain again, then leave to one side. Meanwhile, heat 1 tablespoon of the oil in a small frying pan over a medium-high heat and fry the tofu for 5–10 minutes, turning occasionally, until golden on all sides.

While the tofu fries, heat a wok or large saucepan over a medium heat. Add the sesame seeds and dry-fry for 2–3 minutes, stirring continuously, until just beginning to brown. Tip the sesame seeds on to a plate and leave to one side.

Pour the remaining oil into the wok and add the shallots. Fry for 2–5 minutes until softened. Add the rice vinegar, mirin and miso, and tip in the tofu from the frying pan.

Pour in 1l/35fl oz/4 cups water. Bring to the boil, then reduce the heat to a simmer. Add the pak choi and mushrooms, then immediately remove from the heat.

Divide the udon noodles into serving bowls. Put the pak choi, mushrooms and tofu on top of the noodles, then cover with the miso and enoki liquor. Sprinkle with the toasted sesame seeds and add the chives, then serve.

Gluten-free   *Soya-free*   *Nut-free*   *Seed-free*   *Sugar-free*

spicy lentil & quinoa risotto

Serves: 4
Preparation: 15 minutes
Cooking: 1 hour

1 tbsp olive oil or coconut oil
1 onion, finely chopped
2 garlic cloves, crushed
1cm/½in piece fresh root
  ginger, peeled and grated
1cm/½in piece fresh
  turmeric, peeled and grated
  or ½ tsp ground turmeric
1 tsp ground cumin
1 tsp garam masala
2 tsp crushed chillies
1 red chilli, deseeded and
  thinly sliced
180g/6¼oz tomatoes,
  chopped
300g/10½oz potatoes, cut
  into cubes
250g/9oz/1 cup red lentils,
  rinsed and drained
875ml/30fl oz/3½ cups
  vegetable stock, plus extra
  if needed
100g/3½oz/½ cup red or
  white quinoa, rinsed and
  drained
60g/2¼oz broccoli florets,
  cut in half
120g/4¼oz kale, roughly
  chopped
4 tbsp lemon juice
1 handful of chopped
  coriander leaves
dairy-free yogurt, to serve

Heat the oil in a large saucepan over a medium-low heat. Add the onion, garlic, ginger and fresh turmeric, if using, and cook for 5–8 minutes, stirring frequently, until softened.

Add the ground turmeric, if using, the cumin, garam masala, crushed chillies and fresh chilli, and cook for 30 seconds. Add the tomatoes, potatoes, lentils and 625ml/21½fl oz/2½ cups of the stock, and bring to a gentle boil. Reduce the heat and simmer for 30 minutes, or until the liquid is absorbed.

Add 185ml/6fl oz/¾ cup of the stock and the quinoa, and simmer for 10 minutes. Add more stock, if necessary, to avoid the quinoa becoming too dry. Add the broccoli and kale, and continue cooking for 5 minutes, or until the quinoa is tender and translucent. Stir in the lemon juice and coriander, then ladle into serving bowls and top with a large spoonful of dairy-free yogurt.

Soya-free   Seed-free   Sugar-free

hungarian casserole with garlic croutons

Serves: 4
Preparation: 30 minutes
Cooking: 45 minutes

1 tbsp olive oil or coconut oil
4 large potatoes, cut into
  cubes
1 large onion, chopped
1 red pepper, deseeded and
  chopped
1 green pepper, deseeded
  and chopped
1½ tsp caraway seeds
400g/14oz/scant 1⅔ cups
  tinned chopped tomatoes
250g/9oz/1 cup tinned
  butter beans, rinsed and
  drained
250ml/9fl oz/1 cup vegetable
  stock
2 tsp sweet paprika
60g/2¼oz/½ cup walnuts,
  chopped
sea salt and freshly ground
  black pepper
steamed green vegetables, to
  serve

GARLIC CROUTONS
4 slices of stale sourdough
  bread
2 garlic cloves, crushed
extra virgin olive oil

Heat the oil in a large saucepan over a medium heat. Add the potatoes and cook for 8–10 minutes, stirring frequently, until browned all over. Add the onion, peppers and caraway seeds, and cook for a further 10 minutes.

Add the tomatoes, butter beans, stock and sweet paprika, then season with salt and pepper. Simmer for 25 minutes, or until the potatoes are tender.

Meanwhile, to make the croutons, spread the bread with the garlic, then cut into cubes. Put in a bowl and drizzle over the olive oil. Toss to mix, then fry in a non-stick frying pan until golden, turning to brown on all sides.

Ladle the casserole into bowls and top with the walnuts and croutons. Add a grinding of black pepper and serve with steamed green vegetables.

Although this dish, called *fasolakia*, is traditionally served as an accompaniment, I have added cannellini beans to make it into a substantial meal.

greek beans with *tomatoes*

Serves: 4
Preparation: 15 minutes
Cooking: 1 hour

1 tbsp olive oil or rice
   bran oil
1 onion, finely chopped
2 garlic cloves, crushed
900g/2lb 4oz/4 cups tinned
   chopped tomatoes
800g/1lb 12oz/4 cups tinned
   cannellini beans, rinsed and
   drained
2 tbsp chopped dill leaves
2 tbsp thyme leaves
125ml/4fl oz/½ cup
   vegetable stock, plus extra
   if needed
450g/1lb green beans
2 tbsp extra virgin olive oil
crusty bread or cooked
   quinoa, to serve

Heat the oil in a large saucepan over a medium heat. Add the onion and garlic, and cook for 5–8 minutes until softened.

Add the tomatoes and cannellini beans, and stir to combine. Add the dill and thyme, then pour in 125ml/4fl oz/½ cup stock. Stir, then simmer for 40 minutes, stirring occasionally. Add the green beans and cook for 10 minutes, or until they are tender. Add a little more liquid if the mixture catches on the pan. Remove from the heat and drizzle with the olive oil. Serve with crusty bread.

Gluten-free   *Soya-free*   *Nut-free*   *Seed-free*   *Sugar-free*

rustic tart with *spinach pesto*

Serves: 4
Preparation: 30 minutes
Cooking: 1 hour 15 minutes

150g/5½oz sweet potato,
  thinly sliced into rounds
1 baby beetroot, thinly sliced
80g/2¾oz butternut squash,
  peeled and cut into dice
1 carrot, sliced
1 large onion, cut into thin
  wedges
1 tbsp safflower oil or
  sunflower oil
6 asparagus spears
1 sheet of vegan ready-rolled
  puff pastry, defrosted if
  frozen
15 cherry tomatoes, cut in
  half
70g/2½oz/½ cup hazelnuts,
  chopped
green salad, to serve

TOMATO SPREAD
3 tbsp olive oil or melted
  coconut oil
2 garlic cloves
120g/4¼oz/¾ cup drained
  sun-dried tomatoes in oil
1 tsp dried thyme

SPINACH PESTO
100g/3½oz baby spinach
  leaves
1 handful of parsley leaves
2 tbsp extra virgin olive oil
sea salt and freshly ground
  black pepper

Preheat the oven to 200°C/400°F/Gas 6. Put the sweet potato on a baking sheet and add the beetroot, squash, carrot and onion, then drizzle with the oil. Roast for 45 minutes.

Meanwhile, snap off any woody ends from the asparagus stalks at the point where they break easily, then cut the tender spears into short pieces. Leave to one side.

Put all the ingredients for the tomato spread into a blender or food processor and blend until smooth. Leave to one side.

To make the spinach pesto, put all the ingredients in a blender or food processor and process until finely chopped. Add a little water if the mixture is too thick.

After 45 minutes of roasting the vegetables, add the asparagus to the baking sheet and roast for a further 10 minutes. Remove the baking sheet from the oven and leave to one side.

Lay the pastry sheet on a clean baking sheet, and spread with the tomato spread, leaving a 4cm/1½in border. Arrange the vegetables in a pile in the centre of the pastry, and gently fold in the edges to make a pastry border. Scatter over the cherry tomatoes. Bake the tart for 15 minutes, or until the pastry is golden brown. Drizzle the tart with the spinach pesto, then sprinkle with the chopped nuts. Serve with a big green salad.

Gluten-free   Sugar-free

red lentil & beetroot burgers

Serves: 4
Preparation: 20 minutes, plus
** 1 hour chilling (if time),**
** plus making the relish**
Cooking: 35 minutes

130g/4½oz/½ cup red
  lentils, rinsed and drained
1 small beetroot, roughly
  chopped
½ onion, roughly chopped
1 garlic clove, crushed
½ tbsp tamari soy sauce, soy
  sauce or coconut aminos
1 small handful of parsley
  leaves, chopped
1 tsp crushed chillies
  (optional)
½ tsp sweet paprika
3 tbsp coconut milk, plus
  extra if needed
80g/2¾oz/¾ cup gram flour
  or plain flour, plus extra if
  needed
1 tbsp safflower oil, or
  sunflower oil, olive oil or
  coconut oil
sea salt and freshly ground
  black pepper

TO SERVE
4 wholemeal rolls
cos lettuce leaves
sliced large tomato
Tomato Relish (page 48)
pickles

Put the lentils in a saucepan with 1l/35fl oz/4 cups boiling water and return to the boil over a high heat. Reduce the heat to medium and cook for 10–12 minutes until soft. Drain in a colander and leave to one side.

Meanwhile, put the beetroot and onion into a food processor and process until finely chopped. Leave to one side.

Tip the lentils into a large bowl and add the beetroot mixture. Stir together to combine. Put the garlic in a small bowl and add the tamari, parsley, crushed chillies, if using, and paprika. Season with salt and pepper, then stir together to combine. Stir into the lentil mixture.

Pour in 3 tablespoons coconut milk, and half the flour. Stir well and then add the remaining flour. The consistency should be firm enough to hold its shape without being too dry, and this will depend on the liquid quantity from the beetroot. If it is too wet, add more flour, 1 teaspoon at a time. If it is too dry, add more coconut milk, 1 teaspoon at a time. If you have time, chill the mixture in the fridge for 1 hour.

Divide the mixture into 4 and form each into a burger shape. Heat the oil in a non-stick frying pan over a medium-high heat. Cook the burgers in the oil for 5–6 minutes on each side, until lightly golden – you may need to do this in batches. Serve with wholemeal rolls, salad, relish and pickles.

Gluten-free   Nut-free   Seed-free   Sugar-free

spicy warm tempeh salad

Serves 4
Preparation: 20 minutes
Cooking: 10 minutes

3 tbsp tamari soy sauce or
  soy sauce
½ tsp smoked paprika
2 tsp crushed chillies
450g/1lb tempeh, cut into
  cubes
1 tbsp olive oil or safflower
  oil
2 red onions, finely sliced
1 lettuce, leaves chopped
150g/5½oz baby spinach
  leaves
½ red pepper, deseeded and
  sliced
60g/2¼oz/½ cup pitted
  green and black olives,
  sliced
2 plum or vine tomatoes, cut
  into thin wedges
2 avocados, cut in half,
  pitted, peeled and sliced

CHILLI DRESSING
4 tbsp olive oil
2 tbsp lemon juice
1 tbsp chilli sauce
freshly ground black pepper

Put the tamari in a bowl and add the smoked paprika and crushed chillies. Add the tempeh and mix well to combine, then leave to one side. Heat the oil in a non-stick frying pan over a medium heat. Add the tempeh and cook for 5–8 minutes until golden brown.

Meanwhile, put the onions in a large serving bowl and add the lettuce, spinach, pepper, olives, tomatoes and avocados. Gently mix together, taking care not to mash the avocados.

Put all the ingredients for the dressing in a screwtop jar, cover and shake well to combine. (Alternatively, whisk in a small jug.) Serve the tempeh with the salad and drizzle it with the dressing.

This dish is based on an authentic, smoky, vegan gumbo I tasted in the US. Using a slow cooker gives the gumbo a rich sauce and is my preferred method, but you can also make it in a saucepan cooked over a very low heat.

slow-cooked smoky gumbo

Serves: 6
Preparation: 20 minutes
Cooking: 4¼–7¼ hours in a
  slow cooker or 1¾ hours in
  a saucepan

2 tbsp olive oil or coconut oil
1 onion, chopped
3 garlic cloves, crushed
1 red pepper, deseeded and
  thinly sliced
1 green pepper, deseeded
  and thinly sliced
2 celery sticks, thinly sliced
800g/1lb 12oz/3¼ cups
  tinned chopped tomatoes
400g/14oz/2 cups tinned red
  kidney beans, rinsed and
  drained
1 tsp smoked paprika
½ tsp sweet paprika
½ tsp dried thyme
150g/5½oz/¾ cup easy-cook
  short grain brown rice, or
  jasmine or basmati rice
750ml/26fl oz/3 cups
  vegetable stock
sea salt and freshly ground
  black pepper
chopped coriander leaves
  and chilli sauce, to serve

Heat 1 tablespoon of the oil in a non-stick frying pan over a medium heat and cook the onion and garlic for 5–8 minutes until softened. Add the peppers and celery, and cook for a further 5 minutes, stirring frequently.

Meanwhile, if using a slow cooker, preheat it to High. Put the remaining oil in the slow cooker. Transfer the pepper mixture to the slow cooker and add the remaining ingredients. Season with salt and pepper and stir well. Cook for 5–7 hours on Low or 4–6 hours on High until the rice is cooked.

If using a saucepan, heat the remaining oil in a large heavy-based saucepan over a medium heat, then transfer the pepper mixture to the pan. Add the remaining ingredients, season with salt and pepper, and stir well. Bring to the boil, then reduce the heat to very low and simmer very gently for 1½ hours, or until the rice is cooked.

Top up with boiling water if the mixture becomes too dry. The gumbo should look like a thick soup. Scatter over the coriander and serve with the chilli sauce.

Gluten-free *Soya-free* *Nut-free* *Seed-free* *Sugar-free*

Gluten-free Nut-free Seed-free Sugar-free

vegetable slice with chimichurri
& tomato salsa

Serves 4
Preparation: 20 minutes,
  plus 1 hour resting
Cooking: 1 hour

1 tbsp olive oil or safflower
  oil, plus extra for greasing
1 onion, chopped
4 garlic cloves, crushed
2 courgettes, coarsely grated
200g/7oz baby spinach
300g/10½oz firm tofu
80ml/2½fl oz/⅓ cup soya
  milk
2 tsp cornflour or arrowroot
175g/6oz broccoli, chopped
½ red pepper, deseeded
  and chopped
sea salt and freshly ground
  black pepper

TOMATO SALSA
2 large tomatoes, chopped
½ onion, chopped
juice of 2 limes
1 large handful of coriander
  leaves, chopped

CHIMICHURRI
4 tbsp parsley leaves
1 garlic clove
½ tsp dried oregano
2 tbsp olive oil
1 tsp vinegar
¼ tsp crushed chillies

To make the salsa, put all the ingredients in a serving bowl and add a pinch of salt. Mix well and leave to one side for 1 hour for the flavours to develop.

Preheat the oven to 180°C/350°F/Gas 4 and grease a 23 × 23cm/9 × 9in non-stick baking tin with a little oil. Heat the oil in a non-stick saucepan over a medium heat. Add the onion and garlic, and cook for 5–8 minutes until softened. Add the courgettes to the pan, stir well and cook for 5 minutes, stirring occasionally.

Put the spinach in a blender or food processor and add the tofu, milk and cornflour, then process until smooth. Add the courgette and onion mixture, the broccoli and red pepper. Season with salt and pepper, then pulse quickly to combine roughly, leaving some noticeable pieces of pepper and broccoli.

Pour the mixture into the prepared tin and bake for 45 minutes, or until firm and golden. Meanwhile, to make the chimichurri, put the parsley in a food processor and add the remaining ingredients. Blend until they form a paste. Spoon into a serving bowl and leave to one aside. Serve the vegetable slice with the chimichurri and salsa.

Desserts

The part of the meal I look forward to the most – desserts!
I love making them too, not just for the burst of sweetness
but for the chance to experiment with new flavours and
techniques. Here, I have made traditional desserts with
a fresh twist, and healthier versions of time-honoured
favourites. Brighten your palate with a fruit granita or
sorbet, such as Strawberry & Hibiscus Flower Granita, or
finish your meal with the creamy texture of Coconut Kulfi
Ice Cream or Rosewater & Pistachio Syllabub. Transform a
fresh fruit salad with a touch of Thai by making Fruit Salad
with Strawberry & Lemongrass Syrup or liven up pineapple
by making Griddled Chilli Pineapple with Mint & Yogurt.
And for a twist on a traditional cheesecake, try my Raw
Chocolate Torte with Salted Pecan Sauce.

Lavender Panna Cotta
(page 163).

Hibiscus flower tea is drunk as a traditional herbal remedy in several countries – in Egypt to support a healthy heart and nervous system, in Mexico as a diuretic, in Asia to help lower cholesterol and in the Middle East to relieve restlessness. It has a beautiful scent and flavour, and it complements the flavour of strawberries perfectly in this sweet granita.

strawberry & *hibiscus flower granita*

Serves: 6
Preparation: 5 minutes,
  plus 15 minutes infusing,
  cooling, 10 minutes chilling
  and 2½ hours freezing

2 tbsp dried hibiscus
  flower tea
600g/1lb 5oz strawberries,
  hulled, plus extra
  strawberries, cut in half, to
  decorate
2 tbsp lime juice
1 tbsp brown rice syrup or
  agave syrup
1 tsp syrup from a jar of
  hibiscus flowers (optional)

Put the hibiscus flower tea in a bowl and add 375ml/13fl oz/ 1½ cups boiling water. Leave to infuse for 15 minutes, then leave to cool and chill in the fridge for 10 minutes.

Put the tea into a blender or food processor and add the strawberries, lime juice and brown rice syrup. Blend well. Add the hibiscus syrup, if using, then blend briefly to mix.

Pour into a shallow freezerproof container. Put in the freezer for 30 minutes, then scrape the mixture with a fork to break up the ice crystals slightly.

Repeat the freezing and scraping a further 4 times, or until the granita is frozen throughout with fine, even crystals. Serve in glasses and top with halved strawberries.

Gluten-free *Soya-free* *Nut-free* *Seed-free* *Raw*

lychee, raspberry & *rose sorbet*

Serves: 6
Preparation: 15 minutes,
  plus 4 hours freezing and
  20 minutes defrosting

400g/14oz tinned lychees in
  syrup
140g/5oz/1 cup raspberries
1 tsp rose water
basil leaves, to serve
  (optional)

Put the lychees and their syrup into a blender or food processor
and add the remaining ingredients. Blend until smooth. Pour into
a shallow freezerproof container and put into the freezer for
2 hours, or until the mixture is frozen around the edges.

Using an electric whisk, a blender or food processor, whisk to
break up the crystals, then refreeze for another 1 hour, or until
crystals form. Whisk again and freeze until solid. Defrost at room
temperature for 20 minutes before serving with basil, if you like.

Gluten-free *Soya-free* *Nut-free* *Seed-free*

plum, black pepper & *vanilla sorbet*

Serves: 4
Preparation: 15 minutes, plus
  overnight and an additional
  4 hours freezing and
  20 minutes defrosting

6 ripe, sweet, dark plums,
  pitted and cut into quarters
½ vanilla pod
½ tsp black peppercorns

Put the plums in a freezer bag, seal and freeze overnight.

Split the vanilla pod in half lengthways and scrape out the seeds.
Reserve the pod for another use. Put the vanilla seeds, plums and
peppercorns into a blender or food processor and blend until
smooth and creamy. Serve immediately, or freeze for 3–4 hours
to harden. Defrost at room temperature for 20 minutes and
blend briefly before serving.

Gluten-free *Soya-free* *Nut-free* *Seed-free* *Sugar-free* *Raw*

coconut kulfi ice cream (pictured)

Serves 4
Preparation: 15 minutes,
plus 4 hours freezing

800ml/28fl oz/scant 3½ cups
  coconut cream
4 tbsp coconut oil, melted
180g/6¼oz/1 cup brown
  sugar or coconut sugar
80g/2¾oz/½ cup pistachio
  nuts, plus extra chopped
  pistachio nuts to serve
1 tsp ground cardamom

Put all the ingredients into a blender or food processor and blend until smooth. Pour into a shallow freezerproof container and freeze for 3–4 hours or until almost solid.

Return to the blender and blend until smooth. (Alternatively, pour into an ice-cream maker and follow the manufacturer's instructions.) Serve topped with nuts.

Gluten-free   Soya-free   Seed-free

raw maple pecan ice cream

Serves 4
Preparation: 10 minutes,
plus overnight freezing

4 ripe bananas, chopped
1 vanilla pod
75g/2½oz/½ cup raw
  almond butter
120g/4¼oz/½ cup raw tahini
250g/9oz/¾ cup maple
  syrup or 140g/5oz/¾ cup
  brown sugar or coconut
  sugar
1 tsp ground cinnamon
150g/5½oz/1½ cups pecan
  nuts, chopped

Unless you have an ice-cream maker, put the banana pieces in a freezer bag, seal and freeze overnight.

Split the vanilla pod in half lengthways and scrape out the seeds. Reserve the pod for another use. Put all the ingredients into a high-speed blender or food processor and blend until smooth. (Alternatively, process all the ingredients in a blender or food processor until smooth, then transfer to an ice-cream maker and follow the manufacturer's instructions.) Serve immediately.

Gluten-free   Soya-free   Raw

A traditional Italian dessert, panna cotta is normally made with milk, cream and gelatine. My version, with its delicate floral flavour, is a delicious, light and creamy dessert that you wouldn't believe is vegan. If you have never cooked with agar-agar – the vegetarian alternative to gelatine – before, it's very easy to use and has no taste or colour.

lavender panna cotta

Serves: 4
Preparation: 10 minutes
Cooking: 15 minutes, plus
  cooling and overnight
  chilling

1 vanilla pod
2 tsp culinary lavender
  flowers
500ml/17fl oz/2 cups
  coconut milk
2 tbsp brown sugar or
  coconut sugar
½ tsp ground cinnamon, plus
  extra for sprinkling
2 tsp agar-agar flakes

Split the vanilla pod in half lengthways and scrape out the seeds. Reserve the pod for another use. Using the back of a spoon, crush the lavender flowers.

Put the coconut milk in a small saucepan over a low heat and add the vanilla seeds, lavender, sugar and cinnamon. Bring gently to the boil, then simmer. Add the agar-agar and 2 tablespoons water, and continue to simmer until the agar-agar has dissolved completely and no trace of the flakes can be seen when you lift up some of the mixture in a spoon.

Divide the mixture into four individual ramekins or small glasses. Leave to cool, then put into the fridge to set overnight. Serve sprinkled with cinnamon.

Gluten-free   *Soya-free*   *Seed-free*

A syllabub is an old-fashioned dessert that is traditionally made with cream and wine. It's like a beautifully creamy mousse. My vegan version is just as rich, but it's healthier and made with coconut cream, pistachio nuts and cashew nuts with the delicate flavour of rosewater.

rosewater & *pistachio syllabub*

Serves: 4
Preparation: 15 minutes,
  plus overnight chilling
  and soaking

250ml/9fl oz/1 cup coconut cream in the unopened carton or tin
230g/8oz/1½ cups cashew nuts
80g/2¾oz/½ cup pistachio nuts, plus chopped pistachio nuts to serve
1 tbsp brown sugar or coconut sugar
1–2 tsp rosewater
rose petals, to serve

Chill the coconut cream overnight in the fridge, making sure the carton is upright. Put the cashew nuts in a bowl, cover with water and leave to soak overnight. Drain in a colander, then rinse well and drain again.

Put the pistachio nuts into a food processor and grind until fine but without becoming oily. Leave to one side.

Without shaking the carton of coconut cream, open it and scoop off 100g/3½oz/½ cup of the cream from the top – it will be very, very thick. Put 4 tablespoons of the liquid from the carton in a small bowl. Store the remaining cream and liquid in a covered container in the fridge for another use.

Put the coconut cream into a blender or food processor and add the cashew nuts, sugar and rosewater to taste. Blend until smooth. Add the reserved liquid, 1 tablespoon at a time, if needed, to make the cream soft but thick enough to hold its shape. Pour into a bowl and add the ground pistachio nuts. Spoon into four glasses, and serve sprinkled with chopped pistachio nuts and rose petals.

Gluten-free   Soya-free   Seed-free

Gluten-free   Soya-free   Seed-free

fruit salad with strawberry & lemongrass syrup

Serves: 4
Preparation: 20 minutes
Cooking: 5 minutes, plus
  5 minutes cooling

180g/6¼oz/1 cup brown
  sugar or coconut sugar
2 lemongrass stalks, outer
  leaves removed, bruised
  with a knife
150g/5½oz/1 cup
  strawberries, hulled
2 tsp lime juice
1 banana, sliced
2 kiwi fruits, peeled and cut
  into small dice
150g/5½oz watermelon,
  cut into cubes
150g/5½oz cantaloupe
  melon, cut into cubes
150g/5½oz/1 cup seedless
  green grapes
250ml/9fl oz/1 cup coconut
  cream

Put 375ml/13fl oz/1½ cups water in a small saucepan over a medium heat and add the sugar, lemongrass and strawberries. Bring gently to the boil, then reduce the heat to low and simmer for 4–5 minutes, stirring occasionally, until the sugar is dissolved.

Remove the lemongrass and mash the strawberries using a fork. Whisk in the lime juice, then leave to cool for 5 minutes.

Put the banana slices in a serving bowl and add the kiwi fruit, watermelon, cantaloupe melon and grapes. Add the strawberry and lemongrass syrup, and stir gently to combine. Serve drizzled with coconut cream.

Serve these spiced pears with creamy coconut yogurt or slice them and serve for breakfast to top the Toasted Granola on page 36. You can also slice or dice the pears before cooking, if you prefer.

chai-poached pears

Serves: 6
Preparation: 10 minutes
Cooking: 1 hour

140g/5oz/¾ cup brown
 sugar or coconut sugar
1 tbsp lemon juice
1 tsp cardamom pods,
 crushed
3 cloves
2 cinnamon sticks
1 star anise
½ tsp grated nutmeg
a pinch of sea salt
3 medium pears, peeled,
 stalks intact
dairy-free yogurt, to serve

Put the sugar in a medium saucepan and add 250ml/9fl oz/ 1 cup water, the lemon juice, spices and salt. Bring to just boiling over a medium heat and then reduce the heat to a simmer. Stir well to dissolve the sugar. Turn the heat to low, and add the pears, stirring well to ensure the syrup covers them. Top up with water to cover if necessary. Cook for 30 minutes, or until the pears are tender – the cooking time will depend on the ripeness of the pears.

Remove the pears with a slotted spoon. If you like, you can reduce the remainder of the chai syrup by increasing the heat after the pears have been removed, and cooking for a further 15–25 minutes until thick. Serve the pears with yogurt, and with the reduced juice drizzled over the top, if you like.

Gluten-free Soya-free Nut-free Seed-free

Gluten-free Soya-free

griddled chilli pineapple
with mint & yogurt

Serves: 4
Preparation: 15 minutes
Cooking: 15 minutes

1 large pineapple
2 tbsp brown sugar or
 coconut sugar
½ hot red chilli, such as
 bird's eye, deseeded and
 finely chopped
1 tsp ground cinnamon
1 tbsp safflower oil, sunflower
 oil or coconut oil
a few small mint leaves
250ml/9fl oz/1 cup dairy-free
 coconut yogurt

Cut the top and bottom off the pineapple and stand it up on a chopping board. Slice off the skin, cutting downwards from top to bottom. Carefully cut out any pieces of skin left on the fruit. Cut the pineapple in half lengthways and then in half again, then slice off the woody core so that you are left with the soft fruit. Slice each quarter in half lengthways.

Put the sugar, chilli and cinnamon in a small saucepan over a medium-low heat, and heat through to dissolve the sugar.

Heat a large, ridged griddle over a medium-high heat. Brush both sides of the pineapple with the oil and cook the pineapple in the griddle for 5–6 minutes, turning once, until it is warmed through and is marked with golden lines. You may have to do this in batches. Remove from the griddle and keep warm.

Meanwhile, increase the heat under the saucepan to medium-high to lightly caramelize the sugar. Transfer the pineapple to serving plates, pour the sauce over the top and scatter over the mint leaves. Serve with the yogurt.

Gluten-free   Soya-free   Seed-free   Raw

raw chocolate torte with
salted pecan sauce

Serves: 8
Preparation: 30 minutes
  plus overnight soaking,
  4–5 hours freezing and
  20 minutes defrosting

310g/11oz/2 cups cashew
  nuts
1 vanilla pod
125g/4½oz/⅔ cup coconut
  sugar
125g/4½oz/1 cup raw cacao
  powder
½ tsp sea salt
170ml/5½fl oz/⅔ cup
  coconut oil, melted
raw chocolate shavings and
  mixed berries, to serve

SALTED PECAN SAUCE
180g/6½oz/1 cup fresh or
  dried medjool dates, pitted
100g/3½oz/1 cup pecan nuts
4 tbsp agave syrup or brown
  rice syrup
1 tsp sea salt

DATE BASE
100g/3½oz/½ cup fresh or
  dried medjool dates, pitted
225g/8oz/1½ cups almonds
a pinch of sea salt

Put the cashew nuts in a bowl, cover with water and leave to soak overnight. Drain in a colander and rinse. Put the dates and pecan nuts for the sauce in a bowl. Put the dried dates, if using, for the crust into another bowl. Cover both with water, and leave to soak for 4 hours. Drain and rinse the nuts. Drain the dates for the base, but drain and reserve the date liquid for the sauce.

To make the base, put the almonds, dates and salt into a blender or food processor and blend at high speed to form a soft dough. Press the dough lightly into the base of a 20cm/8in springform cake tin and leave to chill in the fridge while you make the filling.

Split the vanilla pod in half lengthways and scrape out the seeds. Reserve the pod for another use. Put the vanilla seeds, sugar, cacao powder, salt and oil into a blender or food processor and add 185ml/6fl oz/¾ cup water. Blend until smooth. Pour this filling over the base. Freeze the cake for 4–5 hours until firm.

To make the sauce, put all the ingredients into a blender or food processor and blend until smooth, adding the reserved date liquid, 1 tablespoon at a time until the sauce is thick and creamy. Remove the torte from the freezer, then carefully release the tin and slide the torte on to a serving plate. Leave for 20 minutes to defrost slightly. Drizzle the sauce over the top and scatter over the chocolate shavings and mixed berries, then serve.

A fast and easy dessert made with little mouthfuls of chocolate melted through banana in a rice wrapper.

chocolate banana wontons

Serves: 6
Preparation: 25 minutes
Cooking: 20 minutes

1 pack of 30 egg-free vegan wonton wrappers
2 large ripe bananas, chopped
80g/2¾oz dark vegan chocolate, chopped, plus extra chocolate, grated, to serve
4 tbsp safflower oil, sunflower oil or coconut oil, plus extra if needed

Preheat the oven to 100°C/200°F/Gas ½ and put a large heatproof plate inside to warm. Separate the wonton wrappers and lay them on a damp tea towel. This will prevent them from drying out.

Put the bananas in a large bowl and add the dark chocolate, then mix together well. Spoon a small teaspoonful of the banana mixture on to each wonton wrapper. Moisten the edges with a little water and fold into a triangle. Leave on the damp tea towel and continue until all the wonton wrappers are used.

Heat 2 tablespoons of the oil in a large, non-stick frying pan and cook 2 or 3 wontons at a time, allowing them to turn golden brown and bubble a little on the surface. Remove with a slotted spoon and drain on kitchen paper. Keep the wontons warm while you cook the remainder, adding oil as necessary. Serve sprinkled with grated chocolate.

Nut-free

Gluten-free   Soya-free   Seed-free

banana-leaf mango *rice cakes*

Serves: 4
Preparation: 20 minutes
Cooking: 40 minutes, plus
   20 minutes cooling

200g/7oz/1 cup glutinous
   (sticky) rice
250ml/9fl oz/1 cup coconut
   milk, plus extra to serve
½ tsp sea salt
50g/1¾oz/¼ cup brown
   sugar or coconut sugar
2 bananas, chopped
1 small mango, peeled and
   pitted, flesh chopped (about
   80g/2¾oz flesh)
450g/1lb banana leaves,
   defrosted if frozen (8 leaves)
   (or use foil, if unavailable)
black sesame seeds, to serve

Put the rice in a saucepan over a medium-high heat and add the coconut milk, 250ml/9fl oz/1 cup water, the salt and sugar. Stir together, then bring to the boil. Reduce the heat to low and cook for 20 minutes, stirring frequently, or until the rice is plump and the liquid is absorbed. Remove from the heat and leave to cool for 20 minutes.

Preheat the oven to 200°C/400°F/Gas 6 and line a baking tray with baking parchment. When the rice is cool enough to handle, add the bananas and mango to the pan and gently stir to combine.

Lay a banana leaf out flat and take a large tablespoonful of the rice mixture. Form it into a ball and put it on to the banana leaf near to the top edge. Roll up the banana leaf, tucking in the sides neatly. Tie some kitchen string around the banana roll to hold it securely, then put the roll on the prepared baking tray. (Alternatively, grease a small rectangle of foil with a little oil and wrap the rice up as before, sealing the edges well.) Repeat with the remaining rice and banana leaves.

Cook in the oven for 15–20 minutes until the banana leaf starts to turn black. Remove each parcel with tongs and put on to a serving plate, then cut off the string. Serve the rice cakes in the banana leaves (but take the rice out of the foil for serving). Be careful of the steam when opening the parcels. Sprinkle each rice cake with sesame seeds. Enjoy straight from the oven with extra coconut milk drizzled over the top, or serve cooled.

index

Acknowledgements

I would like to thank my dear husband Paul for eating my creations, and even though your two least favourite dishes are soup and curry, you still eat them with love and appreciation – thank you my love. I would also like to thank my parents, Shirley and Steven, for instilling a love of good food in me from a young age, and for being amazing home cooks. Thanks to Charlie and Hank, my fur-babies, for eating everything with gusto (even the failed attempts), and to Grace, Manisha and my editor, Jan, at Duncan Baird Publishers, for holding my hand through this entire process – thank you infinitely. But most of all, thank you to all the Vegie Heads, my followers, fans, sounding boards and friends. Thank you for being you. This book proves that loving what you do, and doing what you love, can change the world.